TODAY'S TEENAGER

Navagating and Mastering Mental Health in a Digital Era

A GUIDE TO UNDERSTANDING AND
SUPPORTING TEEN MENTAL HEALTH

TEEN MENTAL HEALTH

HEIDI R. CROW

Table of Contents

INTRODUCTION

Imagine you're scrolling through social media, just checking out what's going on with your friends and family. Then, you see a post from a teenager. It seems harmless at first; it's just a regular picture of their day. But as you read the comments, you feel a pang of sadness. Mixed in with the likes and emojis are mean words from people hiding behind their screens, making the teen feel bad about themselves. It's a reminder of how tough the online world can be for teens. They face cyberbullying and a ton of pressure to fit in. It makes you think about your own child and how you can help them navigate through all of this while they're online.

Parenting in today's digital world can feel really tough. We often feel unsure and lost, especially when it comes to dealing with our teenagers' feelings, behaviors, and mental health. Teens can be so unpredictable, and it's hard to keep up with what they need. Sometimes, we worry that we might miss signs that they're struggling, which makes us feel guilty and like we're not doing a good job as parents.

Talking to our kids can be really hard too, especially about serious stuff like mental health or social media. We want to connect with them, but it's tough when these topics come up. It can make our relationships with our teens strained and distant. On top of that, there's so much pressure from society to be perfect parents, teachers, or coaches. It feels like we're juggling so much, and it's easy to feel overwhelmed. Guiding teenagers through all of this can feel like an uphill battle.

Amidst these challenges, think about it: What has triggered you to seek help? Was it a late-night conversation with your teenager that left you feeling more confused than ever? Or perhaps an unsettling incident at school that made you question your ability to understand and support your child in this digital era? Whatever the reason, it is the moment of realization that you need guidance and support that matters. I understand your pain, confusion, and frustration. I have been in the same situation. Just remember: You are not alone.

You should know that the digital age has ushered in a new era; one where the dynamics of teenage life are hugely connected to social media, online interactions, and rapidly evolving cultural norms. This book is the guide you need that understands your struggles. It is the beacon of light in the often-confusing journey of supporting and nurturing the mental health of teenagers.

Reading this book will help you understand how the mental health of teens is affected by the digital world we live in. You'll learn practical tips to support teens and communicate better with them, making it easier for you to handle the challenges they face. Plus, you'll get understanding and support for your own worries and difficulties, which will make you feel more confident in your role as a mentor or supporter. You'll also pick up some great ways to talk to teens about important stuff like mental health and social media, which will strengthen your relationship with them.

But don't just take my word for it. Penélope Cruz, renowned actress and mother, has shared her concerns about the impact of technology on children and teenagers. In a CBS Sunday Morning appearance, Cruz expressed her decision not to give phones to her kids for a very long time. She emphasized the need to protect their mental health. She stated, "It's so easy to be manipulated, especially if you have a brain that is still forming. And who pays the price? Not us, not our generation who, maybe at 25, learned how a BlackBerry worked. It's a cruel experiment on children, on teenagers." Cruz's stance echoes the sentiment shared by many of us. She highlighted the lack of protection for developing brains exposed to excessive technology, addressing issues like bullying and the distortion of self-perception.

As the author of this book, I am a fellow traveler on this challenging journey. I understand the complexities of the digital age and the unique challenges it presents in supporting teen mental health. My authority comes from personal experiences and struggles I have faced in my own journey as a mother, caregiver, and mentor.

Before the dawn of this new information, I too struggled with the difficulties of understanding and supporting teenagers in the digital era. It was a path filled with uncertainty, trial, and error. The realization that a comprehensive guide was needed became my driving force. This book is the culmination of years of research, experience, and the quest for a better understanding of how we can handle the delicate terrain of teen mental health amidst the digital revolution.

When you read this book, you're taking a big step toward understanding and helping teens with their mental health. It gives you the tools and confidence to make a real difference in their lives and communities. This isn't just any book; it's like a guide for those who want to support teenagers better. So, why wait? If you ever feel unsure or lost when it comes to understanding teens, this book is for you. Come along on this journey with me and learn how to be the mentor and support system that young people need today.

The Modern Teenager: Understanding Today's Youth

Technology is anything that wasn't around when you were born. –Alan Kay

Understanding the Shift: From Past to Present

Let's travel back in time, into the pre-digital era. It's the time before the internet and this pervasive digital technology. What challenges did the teens of those days face? How did they live their life? What occupied their time? There are many questions you may ask yourself. What you should know is that these teens had their own unique set of pressures and challenges. These challenges were shaped by their societal norms and cultural influences. Though some of the challenges are similar, they are worse in this current era because technology made them worse.

Before the digital age, teenagers struggled with traditional stressors like academic pressure, family expectations, and the quest for social acceptance. The absence of instant connectivity limited the scope of social comparison primarily to local circles. This reduced the external influences on the teens. The emphasis was mainly on face-to-face communication and the challenges were more localized, reflecting the immediate social and familial environments.

During this time, societal expectations were the biggest influence on their mental health. Conformity to established gender roles, academic success, and adherence to cultural expectations were paramount. The pressure to meet these standards often led to feelings of inadequacy and stress among adolescents. The limited exposure to different perspectives of life and information contributed to a more controlled environment, with fewer external factors that could affect teen mental health for those who didn't fit the mold.

Cultural influences were also significant in shaping the expectations and challenges the teens faced. Beliefs, values, and social practices within a given culture greatly influenced the mindset and behaviors of the teenagers. The absence of the constant connectivity prevalent in the digital era meant that the influence of culture was more localized and less susceptible to rapid changes.

In your teen years, do you remember how you lived your life then? Now, try to compare it to how your teens live theirs. Do you think the limited exposure to external influences contributed to a more stable mental health environment, or did it exacerbate existing challenges by limiting avenues for self-expression?

Rise of Digital Influence

If you answered the previous question, you now know the effect of digitalization teens. They no longer live the happy and face-to-face life that we lived back then. Digitalization has changed every aspect of the life of teens.

- **Identity, self-esteem, and body Image**

In today's digital age, teenagers' perceptions of themselves are deeply linked with their online presence. Social media platforms have become virtual mirrors, reflecting back curated images and narratives that have shaped their self-identity. This constant exposure to idealized representations and comparisons with other people on the internet has distorted the way they view their own body image and worth. As teens scroll through carefully crafted feeds, they may internalize unrealistic standards of beauty and success, which impacts their self-esteem. The pressure to conform to these digital ideals has made them feel insecure. Digitalization has been significant in shaping how teens perceive themselves, influencing their sense of identity, self-worth, and body image in significant ways.

- **Relationship development**

The surge in smartphone usage and the prevalence of social media platforms have fundamentally changed how teenagers form and sustain relationships. Digital communication is now a big part of their interactions. This seems to have replaced the face-to-face engagements. While digitalization offers a wider scope for connections, it introduces challenges related to genuine emotional bonds and authentic communication. The shift towards online platforms may provide quantity in terms of connections, but it also poses the risk of diluting the quality of these relationships, raising questions about the depth of emotional understanding in a world dominated by digital communication.

- **Lack of empathy**

The constant connectivity facilitated by digital devices could be a double-edged sword, potentially leading to a decline in empathy among teenagers. The online environment sometimes leads to a detachment from the real emotions of others. Text-based communication, prevalent in digital exchanges, lacks the nuances of face-to-face conversations such as tone, facial expressions, and body language. This absence of non-verbal cues may contribute to a shallower understanding of others' emotions, potentially resulting in a reduced capacity for empathy, particularly in situations where physical presence is absent.

- **Emotion development**

The pervasive influence of technology has left an indelible mark on how adolescents struggle with and express their emotions. Social media platforms act as a public stage for emotional expression. This has enabled teenagers to share their feelings with a broad audience. However, this exposure comes with potential consequences, contributing to emotional volatility. The instant and often public nature of online interactions can impact emotional development, raising concerns about the long-term effects on mental well-being. The digital age brings new dimensions to how teenagers go about their emotions, demanding a critical examination of the evolving relationship between technology and emotional health.

Cultural and Societal Changes

As previously mentioned, teen mental health is greatly influenced by cultural and societal norms. And the changes in these norms reshape the mental health narratives.

- **Family background:** Changes in family structures, such as single-parent households or dual-income families, affect the support systems available to teens.

- **Religion:** Religious beliefs and practices can significantly affect the mental health narratives of teenagers. The changing nature of religious affiliations and the extent to which religious communities provide support contribute to how teens are coping.

- **Social norms:** Societal expectations and norms have a great impact on how teens perceive and address mental health issues. Evolving attitudes towards topics like therapy, seeking help, and expressing vulnerability shape the narrative.

- **Traditions:** Cultural traditions, rituals, and rites of passage contribute to the mental health narratives of teenagers. The preservation or modification of these traditions can affect how teens go about challenges and transitions.

- **Cultural competence in mental health care:** The accessibility and effectiveness of mental health care are influenced by cultural competence. Examining how mental health professionals cater to diverse cultural backgrounds ensures that the support offered aligns with the unique needs of teenagers. Cultural competence fosters an environment where teens feel understood and supported in their mental health journeys.

Navigating the Digital Era: Challenges and Realities

Over the past two decades, our communication methods have transformed, influencing our lifestyles significantly. Previously, we would check if someone was home by calling them, and if not, postpone the conversation. Today, instant connectivity allows us to reach anyone instantly through various means. While this has numerous advantages, the drawbacks of constant digital connection on our lives should not be overlooked.

Our smartphones, now an integral part of us, enable constant communication through text and instant messaging. This perpetual connection also means unfettered access to social media, introducing its own set of consequences. While this digital era has enhanced efficiency in work and facilitated the formation of new friendships and support networks, the downsides of continuous connectivity deserve attention.

24/7 Connectivity

Constant connectivity brings about several psychological implications, impacting your health and mindset.

- **Fuel feelings of addiction:**

You may have the perpetual expectation to always be reachable. This makes you get addicted. The constant need to check messages or notifications makes you dependent on digital interactions, potentially leading to an addictive behavior where you feel compelled to be online at all times.

- **The fear of missing out (FOMO):**

With the presence of social media, there emerges a concern about missing out—an apprehension that others are enjoying their best moments while you might feel left behind. This perception can negatively impact your life. Continuously measuring your experiences against others, particularly through carefully crafted Instagram pictures, doesn't truly reflect anyone's reality. Despite recognizing this reality, you may still find yourself nurturing these emotions, allowing them to evolve into additional sources of anxiety and depression.

- **A stream of negative thoughts:**

On the internet, opinions tend to spread easily. In recent years, there have been notable changes in the political scene. Regardless of your stance, the intense division is prominently evident on social media. This division can result in heated arguments and negative sentiments toward others. Even if you generally stay away from politics, you may still be affected. Additionally, it becomes challenging for you to grasp the true nature of reality when there is an ongoing struggle against fake news, misinformation, and bias.

- **Comparing yourself to others:**

The online world often presents curated and idealized versions of people's lives. Constant exposure to these curated images and lifestyles can lead to unhealthy comparisons. You might find yourself measuring your life against others, potentially diminishing your self-esteem and satisfaction.

- **Failing to live in the moment:**

When your online life mixes too much with your real-life, it can make it hard to enjoy what's happening right now. Always being connected can make it tough to focus on what's happening around you. Instead of being fully present and enjoying real-life stuff, you might be too caught up in what's happening online. This means you could miss out on a lot of cool things going on in the moment. So, try to balance your online time with being present in real life. It's important to enjoy what's happening around you and not let digital stuff distract you too much.

Social Media Influence

Social media, while acknowledged for its potential negative impact on young minds, especially regarding self-esteem, also offers several benefits. As you know, it has already become part of the society, so it's more constructive to guide teenagers in using it responsibly rather than discouraging its use outright. This encourages proper usage and can yield various benefits. Here are some positive effects of social media on teenagers:

- **Strengthened friendships:**

Social media platforms provide teens with a virtual space to nurture and strengthen their friendships. Through constant communication, sharing updates, and engaging in conversations, teens can maintain relationships with friends, whether they are near or far. This continuous interaction builds stronger and more enduring friendships.

- **Reduces feelings of loneliness:**

Social media is like a big online hangout where teens can chat with their friends and find others who are interested in the same things. This helps them feel less lonely because they can connect with people who understand them. They can join groups, talk in group chats, and share things they've experienced. By doing this, they create a supportive online space where they feel like they belong. This makes them feel happier and more emotionally secure.

- **Global awareness and engagement:**

Social media exposes teens to a vast array of information and perspectives from around the world. Through the sharing of news, cultural insights, and diverse opinions, teens can develop a broader global awareness. This exposure encourages them to engage with different cultures, issues, and current events, which leads to a more informed and open-minded worldview. Thus, social media is a tool for global connectivity and understanding.

Well, as mentioned, social media has its bad side too. The negative effects of social media include:

- **Depression:**

Spending excessive time on social media, particularly more than three hours a day, has been associated with an increased risk of teen depression and anxiety. This high risk may be attributed to various factors such as peer pressure, the constant comparison of one's life to others, and the perception of inadequacy when one's life doesn't appear as exciting or fulfilling. Also, it is important to note that victims of cyberbullying are more prone to developing depressive symptoms, which emphasizes the dark side of online interactions.

- **Anxiety:**

The pervasive fear of missing out, commonly known as "FOMO," is a big issue linked to heavy social media use among teens. Constant exposure to friends seemingly enjoying social events without them can lead to feelings of exclusion and loneliness, and this contributes to high anxiety levels. The curated and often idealized online portrayals of others' lives can create unrealistic expectations and standards. This intensifies the anxiety experienced by teens.

- **Body image issues:**

Social media has a big influence on how teenagers see their bodies. When they see lots of pictures that have been changed to look perfect, it can make them feel bad about themselves. They might start to think they need to look a certain way to be beautiful, even if it's not realistic. This can make them do unhealthy things like skipping meals or making themselves sick to try to be thinner. Sometimes, it can even lead to serious problems like anorexia or bulimia, which are eating disorders. Researchers have found that when teenagers spend less time on social media, they start to feel better about their bodies. It shows how much social media can affect how we see ourselves and how we feel inside. So, it's important for teenagers to know that what they see online isn't always real and that they're awesome just the way they are.

Digital Overload

Digital overload happens when you're bombarded with too much stuff from digital devices like phones, tablets, and computers. It's like when you've been staring at screens for so long that your brain feels overwhelmed and tired. You might find yourself using your devices all the time, constantly checking messages, scrolling through social media, and watching videos. It's like your brain is trying to process too much information all at once. This can make you feel stressed, anxious, or even sad because your brain is working overtime. When you're constantly switching between different apps or tasks on your devices, it's called *media multitasking*, and it can make things even worse. Digital overload isn't good for your mental health because it can make you feel exhausted and unable to focus. The following habits can cause digital overload:

- **Spending too much time on devices:**

Excessive screen time, whether on smartphones, computers, or other digital devices, can contribute to digital overload. It hinders healthy activities, disrupts sleep patterns, and can negatively impact physical and mental health.

- **Consuming too much information:**

Teens often face an influx of information from various online sources. Continuous exposure to news, social media updates, and other digital content can lead to cognitive overload, which affects focus, attention span, and overall mental health.

- **Media multitasking:**

Juggling multiple digital activities simultaneously, such as texting while studying or browsing social media during conversations, contributes to media multitasking. This habit not only reduces efficiency but also intensifies cognitive strain.

In response to the challenges posed by digital overload, it becomes crucial to emphasize the following practices:

- **Setting boundaries:**

You should encourage teens to establish limits on screen time and define specific periods for device use. When you do this, you help your child to have a healthier balance between the digital and offline worlds. This prevents the negative consequences associated with excessive digital exposure.

- **Practicing digital detoxes:**

You should introduce scheduled breaks from digital devices, known as *digital detoxes*, in their routines. This allows teenagers to refresh their minds and reduce the adverse effects of continuous online engagement. This intentional disconnection fosters mental well-being and promotes a more mindful approach to technology use.

- **Fostering offline connections:**

If you want to help your friends deal with spending too much time on screens, like phones or computers, you can suggest doing things together in person. That means hanging out face-to-face, going outside for fun activities, or enjoying hobbies that don't involve screens. By doing these things, they can make real connections with people and have more balanced lives. It's like taking a break from screens and enjoying the world around them. This way, they won't feel the bad effects of spending too much time on digital devices.

It's all about finding a healthy balance between screen time and real-life fun!

Statistics and Trends: Unveiling the Truth

In today's digital world, it's important to be careful because social media can introduce some risks to teens. One big issue is that influencers on social media can make teens all act the same. You know those popular people you see on Instagram or TikTok? Well, they set trends that a lot of teens follow. They talk about what's cool, how to dress, and even what to like. This makes teens feel like they have to be like everyone else, instead of being themselves. Because of this, teens end up all looking and acting alike, without much individuality. Since teens really care about what their friends think, they get caught up in these trends quickly. Platforms like TikTok, Instagram, and Pinterest make it easy for these trends to spread fast. So, it's important to keep an eye out for these things. Here are some crucial aspects you need to watch out for:

- **Social comparisons:**

Social media often creates an environment where teens compare their lives with others. This leads to feelings of inadequacy or low self-esteem. You should be aware of signs that the teens might be negatively impacted by such social comparisons and foster healthy discussions about self-worth and individuality.

- **Gendered disinformation and amplified misogyny:**

The internet sometimes perpetuates gender-based disinformation and misogyny. Teens may come across distorted views of gender roles or experience amplified sexism online. You should engage in conversations about online content with your teens, and this promotes critical thinking and reinforces respectful attitudes toward all genders.

- **Cyberbullying:**

You must understand the full extent of cyberbullying, as social media provides bullies with an online space where they can act without accountability. Cyberbullying includes name-calling, threats, spreading rumors, impersonation, and exclusion from peer groups. Its impact on teens is often underestimated, but cases like Amanda Todd's suicide and Victoria Seigel's tragic death highlight its severity. Cyberbullying can lead to moodiness, anxiety, depression, and even suicide. Parents must recognize its serious mental health implications and take proactive measures to address it.

- **Online predators:**

Besides worrying about your child's interactions with other kids, there's the concern of online predators. They come in various guises and can target your children for financial exploitation or sexual solicitation, often under assumed identities. What's particularly alarming is their patience; they prey on emotionally vulnerable children, building rapport over time before exploiting them. While social media fosters connections, it also poses risks that we must remain vigilant against.

- **Inappropriate content:**

Most social media platforms lack clear guidelines for age-appropriate content, favoring freedom of speech. Facebook, Tumblr, and Instagram, with blurred posting boundaries, expose users to potentially inappropriate material like violence, nudity, politics, and pornography. Navigating this vast information flow is challenging for vigilant parents. Parental control apps have become valuable tools, effectively blocking inappropriate content and keeping parents informed about their child's online activities. While uncomfortable, parental initiative is crucial for online safety, preventing potential risks like inappropriate interactions with strangers, ultimately safeguarding children from harm.

- **Oversharing:**

Teenagers often fall into the trap of oversharing on social media, detailing every aspect of their lives, from lunch outings with friends to showcasing new purchases and daily quirks. While seemingly harmless, this practice raises significant privacy concerns. Social media platforms grapple with determining the boundaries of sharing and privacy, leaving users vulnerable. For instance, once posted on Instagram, content becomes the platform's property, making it challenging to prevent reposts or unauthorized use. This lack of control over personal content exposes users to privacy breaches and potential online exploitation, as exemplified by Ruth Palmer's unfortunate experience with an online stalker.

- **Digital kidnapping:**

Digital kidnapping involves the unauthorized use of someone's online identity, often by creating fake profiles or sharing manipulated content. You should educate your child on the significance of protecting their digital identity, using privacy settings, and reporting any instances of identity theft or manipulation.

Social media has gotten a lot of criticism from people all over the world, and there have been many reports saying it can cause serious problems. Studies done by experts across countries have shown that using social media can really mess with your mental health. It's not just a small thing; it can be really bad for some people. These surveys and studies have found that using social media can lead to some really tough times for users' minds and emotions.

In the United States, there has been a big increase, about 25%, in teenagers trying to hurt themselves from 2009 to

2017. This happened around the same time that more and more people started using social media. A study from 2021 found that girls who spend at least two hours every day on social media starting from age 13 are more likely to have serious thoughts about hurting themselves when they become adults (Sherrell, 2021).

Another study looked at a lot of people and found that there's been a 37% increase in teenagers feeling really sad and hopeless for a long time in the U.S. This means more and more teenagers are struggling with big feelings of sadness and hopelessness (Mojtabai et al., 2016).

Also, in 2019, another study found that teenagers who spend more than three hours every day on social media are more likely to have problems with their mental health. This can include feeling really sad, worrying a lot, being angry, or not wanting to be around other people. So, spending too much time on social media might not be good for how you feel inside (Riehm et al., 2019).

Family and Community Involvement

As a parent, you want your child to do well and be happy in life. But life isn't always easy; it throws challenges our way that we might not expect. That's why it's important for us to help our children learn how to handle these challenges and stay mentally healthy. We have a big role in teaching them important skills to deal with tough situations. This means helping them understand their emotions, how to communicate with others, and how to solve problems. Today, with so much technology around, it's even more important to guide them through the digital world's challenges. Supporting our teens' mental health isn't just up to us as parents; it's something that involves our whole family and community. So, by working together, we can help our children grow into strong, resilient individuals who can handle whatever life throws their way.

- **Foster self-acceptance:**

As parents, your role is really important in helping your kids feel good about themselves and believe in their abilities. Encourage them to try new things they enjoy and get better at them, while also showing them how to set goals they can actually reach. When you do this, you're giving them the support they need to figure out how to reach those goals. Your advice and encouragement are like a roadmap for them to feel good about who they are and what they can do. This helps them feel stronger and more sure of themselves when they face tough situations.

- **Discuss difficult emotions:**

To support your teen's emotional well-being, it's important to understand societal expectations and equip them with skills to navigate challenging emotions. Initiate conversations with your child about their feelings, encouraging them to express emotions through creative outlets like art, music, or writing. Regularly check in with your teen, responding empathetically to their disclosures, using phrases like, "I understand," "that sounds challenging," or "that makes sense." Reinforce your availability, assuring them that you're there to listen, regardless of the situation. Pay attention to small details, promoting awareness of your mental and emotional states. Discussing gratitude can also enhance positive well-being, with you sharing what you're thankful for as a parent.

- **Build relationships:**

Research indicates that strong family relationships play a pivotal role in lessening the likelihood of teenagers facing mental health challenges. It's beneficial to motivate your child to forge new friendships and sustain an active connection with existing friends. These connections contribute to a sense of belonging, which is crucial for their well-being. Facilitate the development of meaningful relationships by encouraging their involvement in school activities, sports teams, volunteering, and quality family time. Equipping them with conflict resolution skills in relationships is equally important for fostering their mental health.

- **Encourage healthy coping skills for stress and anxiety:**

When your teen feels frustrated, collaborate with them to find solutions to the issues they're facing. Prompt your child to think about how they can independently resolve conflicts, empowering them to take ownership of their challenges. Additionally, help them recognize that feeling stressed is a common experience, and some stress can be beneficial, enhancing our performance. Discussing the worst-case scenario can provide perspective, showing that even in challenging situations, there are ways to cope and move forward.

- **Ensure sufficient good quality sleep:**

Quality sleep is crucial for maintaining positive mental health. External factors, particularly mobile phones and social media, can significantly impact the quality of sleep. The constant notifications or 'pings' throughout the night can disrupt sleep patterns. When teenagers experience stress or low moods, it can further disrupt their sleep, leading to irregular patterns such as sleeping during the day and staying awake at night. Realigning young people with a consistent circadian sleep pattern can greatly enhance their mental health.

Family expectations, such as restricting technology use in bedrooms, serve as a practical measure for parents to ensure their children attain sufficient and quality sleep. This, in turn, is important in supporting effective learning, sound decision-making, and overall positive well-being.

- **Limit screen time:**

Nowadays, it's become normal for kids to connect virtually through texting, social media, or gaming. However, this online interaction comes with challenges. Online bullying, increased exposure to violence, and unrealistic body images can make it tough for kids to maintain good mental health. Spending too much time on screens leads to problems like inactivity, wasted time that could be spent on schoolwork, difficulty in building face-to-face relationships, and most importantly, a lack of sufficient sleep. For parents, managing screen time has become one of the significant challenges, yet it holds the potential for the most significant impact on their children's mental health.

- **Avoid power struggles:**

In times of uncertainty, teenagers may feel a lack of control over their lives, leading to struggles. Instead of trying to dominate their opinions, it's important to understand their need to assert control. When faced with conflicts, it's best to avoid discussing issues when emotions are running high. Taking a step back, calming down, and addressing the problem later leads to more productive conversations. By managing your emotions and demonstrating this to your teenager, you teach them valuable skills in emotional regulation.

- **Encouraging them to be active:**

Engaging in co-curricular activities, such as sports or dance, both within and outside of school, offers numerous opportunities and is associated with a reduced risk of mental health issues. Encouraging your child to participate in activities aligned with their interests fosters a sense of connection to their school and peers. It not only allows them to develop confidence but also makes them feel valued for their unique abilities. Additionally, being outdoors during these activities contributes significantly to promoting overall well-being, enhancing the positive impact on mental health.

- **Volunteer together:**

Feeling fulfilled and finding purpose comes from dedicating our time and effort to assist others. When we engage in volunteering or invest time in a cause that resonates with our child and demonstrate acts of kindness, it cultivates a sense of empathy within them. Guiding them to contribute to their community ensures they recognize their value and fosters stronger connections with their parents. This shared experience of giving back not only provides a sense of meaning but also reinforces the importance of empathy and community involvement in their lives.

- **Modelling positive mental health:**

Parents are really important in helping schools promote healthy habits for kids. They do this by showing their own kids how to take care of their mental health. This means parents need to take care of themselves too, by managing their stress well and making time for fun things. When kids see their parents doing these things, it teaches them that mental health is important. It shows them that even when things get tough, there are ways to deal with it and bounce back. This teaches kids to be strong and shows them that looking after their mental health is really valuable.

Growing up can be tough for teens. They have to deal with a bunch of different things as they become adults. This might mean feeling stressed about school, figuring out friendships, understanding who they are, and handling all sorts of feelings. Sometimes, they might feel pressure from friends or worry about how they look or feel about themselves. They might even struggle with things like feeling sad or anxious.

In facing these challenges, teenagers often wish that elders and their parents would understand them without judgment or dismissiveness of their feelings. They long for empathy, validation, and support from the adults in their lives. Instead of being met with criticism or invalidation, they seek understanding, open communication, and acceptance of their experiences and emotions. This allows them to feel heard, respected, and valued, ultimately fostering a healthier relationship and promoting their overall well-being.

In conclusion, reflecting on the profound changes in teen mental health dynamics prompts consideration of their significant impact. From the pre-digital era to today's digital age, societal norms and digital influences have shaped challenges for teens. Distorted self-identity on social media and altered relationship dynamics pose challenges for adolescent emotional well-being. Understanding these changes empowers parents to navigate complexities, fostering family and community involvement. Promoting self-acceptance, open discussions, building relationships, and encouraging healthy coping mechanisms are crucial in supporting teen mental health amidst digital challenges.

In the next chapter, you will gain a comprehensive understanding of digital literacy and its importance in today's world.

Today's Landscape: Building Digital Literacy Skills

Digital literacy is the key to navigating the ever-changing digital landscape. –Anonymous

Navigating Digital Literacy

In this current era, important digital literacy is a much-needed skill set. When you have this skill set, you can navigate, understand, and create information online. Digital literacy involves the proficiency to use digital tools and platforms effectively. This enables you to engage with technology, assess information critically, and communicate in diverse digital formats. Digital literacy is made up of different components; they include:

- **Creativity:**

When you're creative, you can make cool stuff using computer programs like Photoshop for making posters or Blender for creating animations. Being creative means you can come up with new and interesting ways to share your ideas and solve problems. So, whether you're designing a poster for a school project or making a fun animation just for fun, being creative helps you express yourself in awesome ways.

- **Critical thinking and evaluation:**

This is where you can analyze and evaluate digital content for its credibility, accuracy, and bias. With this skill, you can critically assess news articles or social media posts to determine their reliability before sharing them. In this era that is full of misinformation and fake news, critical thinking skills can help you make informed decisions and avoid the spread of false information.

- **Cultural and social understanding:**

Understanding different cultural norms and perspectives can help you go about online interactions respectfully and avoid unintentional offense. In a globalized world where people from different backgrounds connect online, cultural and social understanding leads to inclusive and respectful digital communities.

- **Collaboration:**

Digital literacy involves the ability to work effectively with others using digital tools and platforms—collaboration. With this skill, you can collaborate on projects using Google Docs or participating in online forums requires communication and teamwork skills.

- **Find and select information:**

This component entails the ability to locate, evaluate, and use digital information effectively. When you have this skill, you are able to use search engines to find relevant information and assess the credibility of sources. At the moment, there is too much information overload, and the ability to find and select reliable information becomes difficult. Finding reliable information helps you make informed decisions and solve problems effectively.

- **Effective communication:**

Another component is the ability to communicate clearly and persuasively using digital tools such as email, social media, and video conferencing platforms. With this skill, you can build relationships, collaborate with others, and achieve personal and professional goals easily.

- **E-safety:**

This component involves knowledge of how to stay safe and secure online, which includes protecting personal information and avoiding online threats such as phishing scams and cyberbullying. Applying this component helps you safeguard your online identity.

- **Functional skills:**

Digital literacy includes basic skills such as typing, using software applications, and navigating digital interfaces. For example, your proficiency in Microsoft Office or Google Suite enables you to complete tasks efficiently in academic and professional settings. These functional skills are important for engaging with technology effectively and participating fully in modern society.

Adapting to Digital Trends

It's really important to keep up with all the new technology and trends that keep popping up. Technology changes so fast and affects everything from how we talk to each other, learn, do business, and even have fun. When new digital tools and platforms come out, they bring both cool opportunities and tricky challenges that you need to figure out.

Why should you care about all these new tech things? Well, staying in the loop helps you spot chances to do things better and smarter, both in your work and personal life. For businesses, being ahead of the game can mean getting ahead of competitors, finding new customers, and making people happier with what you offer. And for you personally, it means you can find new ways to make tasks easier, learn new stuff faster, and connect with people who matter to you.

Keeping an eye on digital trends also helps you keep up with what people like and want. The world is always changing and so are what people expect from technology. By understanding what's trending, you can make sure your products, services, or content stay fresh and exciting for your audience. Whether it's coming up with new ways to market things online, creating interesting things, or making sure everyone gets a personalized experience, knowing what's hot is super important for success.

Plus, learning about all these new technologies isn't just good for work; it's also great for your personal growth. Nowadays, knowing your way around digital media is super important no matter what job you do. From basic computer skills to more advanced things like coding or understanding data, being comfortable with digital tools makes you more adaptable and valuable in today's job market.

So, how do you keep up with all this? To keep up with all the new technological advances happening, you've got to be ready to learn new things and stay updated. One way to do this is by taking online courses or watching tutorials on sites like Coursera, Udemy, or LinkedIn Learning. They've got tons of information on everything from coding to digital marketing. When you spend time learning regularly, you can pick up new skills and know what's going on in your field, which makes you more valuable at work.

Another idea is to get hands-on experience by doing real projects. You could join hackathons, be part of online groups, or help out with open-source projects. By working with others, you get better at what you do, make useful connections, and learn about new things happening in your area of interest.

And don't forget to stay curious and open-minded. Technology changes fast, so it's important to be flexible and willing to try new stuff. If you're okay with experimenting and not afraid to make mistakes, you'll be better at dealing with changes and finding new opportunities to grow. It might mean doing things that feel a bit scary or different, but that's how you learn and get ahead in the digital world.

Digital Literacy for Everyday Life

Without any doubt, digital literacy has become an essential skill in today's society, impacting various aspects of our daily lives, whether we are conscious of it or not. From professional tasks to personal communication and entertainment, digital literacy is important in enhancing efficiency, convenience, and accessibility.

In your professional life, digital literacy enables you to perform tasks such as job searching, communicating with colleagues and clients, storing and retrieving records, and managing time effectively. Proficiency with Customer Relationship Management (CRM) or Content Management Systems (CMS) allows you to streamline workflows and improve productivity. Also, familiarity with accounting and tax preparation software facilitates financial management tasks, contributing to the smooth operation of your business or career.

Financial transactions have also shifted to digital platforms, requiring digital literacy for activities such as online banking, portfolio management, and using virtual payment methods. Understanding how to navigate these systems safely and securely is essential for managing your finances effectively and protecting your personal information.

When it comes to having fun, being digitally literate means you can enjoy lots of different things online, like watching videos, reading digital books, listening to podcasts, and even editing photos and videos. Knowing how to use these things lets you explore and have a blast while also keeping up with what's happening and expressing yourself creatively.

For staying updated and learning new things, digital literacy is super important. It helps you check out news online, take part in online classes, search for things on the internet, and join webinars or virtual meetings. Being good at these skills opens up tons of opportunities for learning and growing, whether it's for school or your career.

At home, being digitally savvy helps you handle tasks like setting alarms, controlling smart gadgets, and keeping your home safe with digital security systems. Knowing how to use these technologies makes life easier and safer for you and your family every day.

Communication has changed a lot because of digital tools like cell phones, email, texting, online chats, video calls, and social media. Being digitally literate means you can talk with others easily across all these different platforms, keep in touch with friends and family, and understand how to communicate well online.

All in all, digital literacy isn't just about knowing how to use computers or phones; it's a basic skill that helps you do well in the modern world. When you get better at using technology, you can make your work life, friendships, and fun times better too.

Safe Passage: Navigating Online Spaces

You often hear about cyberthreats in the news, with reporters issuing obscure warnings about malware attacks, worms, and phishing scams. But what does all of this mean? Understanding basic cybersecurity terms and concepts will help you decipher news alerts about virus outbreaks. You'll learn about the types of threats issued and the actions you can take to protect your data and devices.

Malware, including viruses, is a broad term referring to any unwanted or destructive software installed on a device or network. While viruses are a type of malware, they're not the only kind. Cybersecurity experts classify malware based on behavior, with viruses being unique in their ability to replicate and spread. Similar to the common cold or flu, computer viruses are transmitted between devices through email attachments or links.

Just as you prioritize raising healthy kids by providing nutritious meals, flu shots, and teaching hygiene practices, protecting your devices from viruses and malware requires a proactive approach. This includes adopting good cybersecurity habits, such as installing antivirus software and practicing online safety measures.

Social Engineering

Social engineering is how cyber thieves manipulate you into unknowingly spreading malware, revealing your personal information, or sharing your data. Children and teenagers are especially susceptible to these tricks. Educating them on good online habits and identifying warning signs keeps them and your devices safe.

You may receive an email or a notification from Facebook titled "Issues with your account: Please respond." It claims the Facebook team found "copyright issues" with your account and threatens to "permanently block" it if not resolved. Concerned, you follow the instructions, clicking the provided link and providing your credentials on a fake Facebook website.

In reality, you've just handed over access to your account to hackers. This scenario illustrates phishing, a common method of identity theft and virus propagation. Phishing emails exploit our emotions and confirmation bias to profit.

To avoid falling victim:

1. Scan emails for correct logos, fonts, and colors.

2. Look for grammatical and spelling mistakes.

3. Hover over links to verify the URL.

4. If unsure, contact the organization directly through their website or phone.

5. Report scams to the Federal Trade Commission's website.

To improve your cybersecurity, follow these practical tips:

- Avoid opening suspicious emails, as they may contain phishing scams or malware.

- Keep your hardware up-to-date to ensure it can support the latest security upgrades.

- Use a secure file-sharing solution for confidential information and install anti-virus and anti-malware software.

- Check links before opening them to avoid phishing attempts.

- Put effort into creating strong passwords and disable Bluetooth when not in use to prevent hacking.

- Remove adware from your devices to protect your privacy.

- Double-check the address (https://) on websites before sharing personal information.

- Store important information in secure locations and scan external storage devices for viruses.

- Avoid the "secure enough" mentality and invest in security upgrades when available.

- Back up important data regularly to prevent loss in case of a security breach.

- Use a web address (https://) on your website to encrypt information.

- Consider hiring a "White Hat" hacker to identify and address security risks proactively.

Privacy Protection Strategies

To safeguard your personal privacy online, adopting effective strategies is important. Here are actionable steps that you can take to protect your privacy on the internet:

- **Use strong and unique passwords:**

Make sure your passwords are strong and different on every platform when you are in charge of your online accounts. To improve security, use a mix of characters, digits, and symbols. Don't use facts that can be guessed at, such birthdays or everyday terms.

- **Enable two-factor authentication:**

By implementing two-factor authentication (2FA) for your accounts, you enhance their security. This additional layer of protection necessitates a secondary verification step, typically involving a code sent to your mobile device, thereby bolstering your account's security even more.

- **Check privacy settings during app updates:**

Whenever you update your apps, take a moment to review and adjust your privacy settings. Apps may introduce new features or modify existing settings, potentially impacting your data privacy. Stay in control by customizing your preferences after each update.

- **Be cautious about social media sharing:**

Limit disclosed personal details like location and contact info. Adjust privacy settings to control profile access.

- **Regularly update software and applications:**

Update your software and programs on a regular basis to fortify your digital defenses. Updates are released by developers to fix vulnerabilities in addition to adding new features. You lower your chance of being taken advantage of by potential cybercriminals by keeping yourself updated.

- **Use a virtual private network (VPN):**

Enhance online privacy with a VPN, encrypting your internet connection for secure and private online activities. Due to the increased risk of unauthorized access, it is mostly important when using public Wi-Fi networks.

Digital Footprint Management

Your digital footprint is the collection of traces and information you leave behind when using the internet. This footprint expands through various online activities, such as posting on social media, subscribing to newsletters, writing online reviews, or making purchases on the internet.

It's not always evident that you're actively contributing to your digital footprint. Websites, for instance, employ cookies that track your online behavior, even when you might not be aware of it. Similarly, applications have the capability to gather and compile your data surreptitiously. When you grant permission for an organization to access your information, there's a risk that they might sell or share your data with third parties. Additionally, in the unfortunate event of a data breach, your personal information could be compromised.

Your digital footprint is a result of both intentional actions, like posting on social media, and unintentional ones, such as allowing websites and apps to collect your data. This trail of information holds significance because it not only reflects your online activities but can also be susceptible to privacy risks and unauthorized sharing of personal data.

Whenever digital footprints are talked about, it's impossible to understand the terms "active" and "passive." What do they mean?

- **Active digital footprints**

An active digital footprint is when you intentionally share information about yourself online. This could happen by posting on social media platforms, participating in online forums, or filling out forms on websites. Essentially, any action where the user actively provides personal information contributes to their active digital footprint. For instance, when you log into a website with a registered username or profile and make posts or comments, you are actively adding to your digital footprint. Similarly, when you subscribe to newsletters or agree to accept cookies on your browser, you are actively contributing to the data collected about you online.

- **Passive digital footprints**

A passive digital footprint is created without the user's direct knowledge or consent. This occurs when information is collected about the user's online activities without their awareness. For example, websites may track users' visits, their geographical location, and their IP address without explicitly notifying them. This process happens in the background, often without users realizing that their actions are being monitored. Additionally, social networking sites and advertisers may gather data about users' likes, shares, and comments to create profiles and deliver targeted content, all without the user actively providing this information.

Digital Footprint Examples

As an internet user, you may have hundreds of items in your digital footprint. You can increase your digital footprint in a number of ways, such as:

Online shopping:

- When you make purchases from e-commerce websites, your transaction history becomes part of your digital footprint.

- Signing up for coupons or creating an account on shopping platforms adds to the information associated with your online identity.

- Downloading and using shopping apps, as well as registering for brand newsletters, contribute to your digital presence.

Online banking:

- Using a mobile banking app to manage your finances leaves a digital trace.

- Engaging in activities like buying or selling stocks, subscribing to financial publications, and opening a credit card account becomes part of your online financial profile.

Social media:

- Your presence on social media, whether on a computer or mobile device, significantly contributes to your digital footprint.

- Using your social media credentials to log into other websites connects those activities to your online identity.

- Connecting with friends and contacts, sharing information, data, and photos with them all shape your digital presence.

- Joining a dating site or app also becomes part of your digital footprint.

Reading the news:

- Subscribing to an online news source or viewing articles on a news app adds to the content associated with your online identity.

- Signing up for a publication's newsletter and reposting articles or information you find interesting contribute to your digital trail.

Health and fitness:

- When you use health applications and fitness trackers to keep an eye on your health, digital records are created.

- Adding your email address to a gym's registration form and following blogs about health and fitness enhances your online health profile.

Tips for Managing Digital Footprints

When you want to manage your digital footprint effectively, you can follow the following tips:

- Search for your name on popular engines to monitor your public information.

- Reduce mentions by being selective about platforms, minimizing non-essential or risky ones.

- Exercise caution in sharing personal data; assess necessity before providing sensitive details.

- Regularly update and review privacy settings on social media and other online accounts.

- Avoid oversharing on social platforms to minimize the impact on your digital footprint.

- Be cautious about website choices, sticking to reputable and secure sites.

- Refrain from sharing private data on public Wi-Fi to mitigate security risks.

- Delete unnecessary accounts to reduce your online presence and associated risks.

- Strengthen security by using complex passwords and a reliable manager.

- Avoid logging in with Facebook to limit shared information across platforms.

- Keep software updated to patch vulnerabilities and enhance digital security.

- Assess mobile app permissions, disabling unnecessary access for reduced digital footprint.

- Take swift action after a security breach, changing passwords and enabling two-factor authentication.

- Enhance online security with a Virtual Private Network (VPN) to encrypt internet connections.

Social Media Mastery

Social media has become part of our daily lives, and it is through it that we communicate, share information, and connect with others. There are several social media platforms that have come up. Each of these platforms cater to different preferences and purposes. The popular social media platforms include:

- **Facebook**

It is one of the pioneers in the social media platforms. It is a versatile platform for connecting with friends and family. Its key features include status updates, photo and video sharing, and the creation of groups and events. However, it's important to be wary of potential privacy risks, as the platform has faced criticism for data breaches and the misuse of personal information.

- **YouTube**

This platform is all about videos. It's made for people who make videos and those who watch them. You can find videos about pretty much anything, from learning new things to just having fun. There are videos that are really long and others that are short and sweet. YouTube is great because it helps people share their ideas and skills with others, and you can learn a lot from watching. But it's also important to be careful because there can be mean comments, videos that aren't suitable for everyone, and spending too much time staring at screens can be bad for you.

- **Instagram**

This a visually-driven platform, which focuses on photo and video sharing. Its key features include filters, stories, and IGTV. Despite leading to creativity and self-expression, Instagram has been linked to issues such as unrealistic beauty standards, cyberbullying, and the pressure to curate a perfect online persona.

- **TikTok**

This app is pretty new, but it's become super popular because of its short videos and trends that spread like wildfire. It's a place where people can show off their creativity, but some worries have come up about privacy and the appropriateness of the content shared on the platform itself. If your teens are on TikTok, it's important to keep an eye on what they're doing to make sure they're safe online.

- **Snapchat**

Snapchat is popular amongst young people because messages disappear after you've seen them. It's all about sharing photos and videos instantly. Snapchat is all about being quick and having a good time, but because things disappear, it can sometimes lead to risky stuff. Some people worry about their privacy when using Snapchat because of this.

- **X/Twitter**

X, which used to be called Twitter, is a place where people post short messages called *tweets*. You can share your thoughts, pictures, or links with others. There are some cool features like hashtags, which help organize topics, retweets, which let you share someone else's tweet, and likes, which show you enjoyed a tweet. Twitter is great for chatting with others right away, but some people don't like it because it can sometimes be a place where people say mean things or share false information.

How does social platforms impact the mental health of teens? Each platform has a unique impact on teen mental health. The constant exposure to curated lifestyles on Facebook and Instagram may contribute to feelings of inadequacy and low self-esteem among teens. YouTube and TikTok, with their emphasis on likes and views, can create a sense of validation tied to online popularity. Snapchat's focus on real-time communication may contribute to anxiety about missing out.

Navigating Social Media Challenges

Even though social media has its good side, it brings along some problems too:

- Online vs. reality: Sometimes, what you see on social media isn't the whole truth. People might act differently online than they do in real life. Plus, not everyone you're "friends" with online is really your friend; some might even be strangers.

- Increased usage: Spending too much time on social media isn't great for you. It can make you a target for cyberbullies, make you feel down, and sometimes, you might see things that aren't suitable for your age. So, it's not a good idea to be on social media too much.

- Social media addiction: Social media is kind of like a game that you can't stop playing or a job you can't finish. When you share something or get likes on your posts, it makes you feel really good because your brain releases happy chemicals like dopamine. This feeling makes you want to keep using social media over and over again, even if you don't notice it happening.

- Fear of missing out (FOMO): Many people worry about missing out on things if they're not online all the time. This can affect their mental health.

- Self-image issues: Social media can make you feel like you need approval for how you look or make you compare yourself to others. This is especially true if you're always posting pictures of yourself. Spending too much time on platforms like Facebook can make some people feel like their worth is tied to how they look. Social media doesn't cause these problems, but it can make them worse by encouraging certain behaviors.

Promoting Positive Social Media Habits

Promoting positive social media habits is important in maintaining a healthy digital lifestyle. To create a more mindful and uplifting online experience, you need to add the following actionable tips into your routine:

- **Take inventory:** Begin by evaluating your current social media usage. Reflect on the platforms you engage with and assess the impact they have on your well-being. Identify any negative patterns or sources of stress.

- **Set limits:** Establish clear boundaries for your social media activity. Define specific timeframes for usage and stick to them. By setting limits, you can prevent the endless scrolling that often leads to excessive screen time and potential negative emotions.

- **Spring clean your accounts:** Regularly review and declutter your social media accounts. Unfollow or mute accounts that contribute to a negative atmosphere and curate your feed to include content that inspires and uplifts you.

- **Start fresh:** Consider starting anew by revisiting your privacy settings and adjusting them to suit your comfort level. This can enhance your control over the information you share and increase your overall sense of security.

- **Create a 1:1 plan:** Develop a personalized plan that aligns with your goals and values. Ensure that your online activities contribute positively to your life, fostering connections and enriching your digital experience.

- **Disrupt your patterns:** Identify recurring habits that may be contributing to a negative social media experience. Intentionally disrupt these patterns by introducing new activities or diversifying your online interactions.

- **Take a break:** Understanding why it's good to take breaks from social media is important. It's like giving yourself a breather so you can feel refreshed and focused again. Stepping away for a bit helps you keep a good balance between being online and enjoying the real world around you.

- **Schedule offline time:** Incorporate dedicated offline time into your daily routine. Whether it's a brief walk, meditation, or quality time with loved ones, scheduling moments away from screens promotes overall health.

- **Limit screen time:** It's a good idea to decide on how long you'll spend looking at screens each day, not just on social media but also on other digital mediums. Doing this can stop bad things from happening because you're not staring at screens too much, which helps you have a more balanced life.

To conclude, equipping yourself with digital literacy skills empowers you to navigate the complexities of the online world effectively. Apply the knowledge gained from this chapter in your interactions with teenagers, emphasizing your role in guiding responsible digital behavior. Encourage creativity, critical thinking, cultural understanding, collaboration, and effective communication to foster a positive online environment. Emphasize e-safety, functional skills, and the importance of adapting to digital trends. Actively manage your digital footprint, prioritize privacy protection, and navigate social media challenges wisely. By embracing these practices, you play a pivotal role in promoting a mindful and positive digital lifestyle for yourself and the teenagers you engage with.

In the next chapter, you will understand the challenges of comparison culture in the digital era and be equipped with practical strategies to navigate and overcome the comparison trap, which would lead to resilience and promoting self-appreciation and mental well-being among teenagers.

The Art of Self-Appreciation: Thriving Beyond Comparison

Comparison is the thief of joy. –Theodore Roosevelt

You should always remember that constantly measuring your achievements against others steals the joy from your unique path. Accept your progress, acknowledging that everyone has their own timeline. Instead of comparing, focus on personal growth, celebrating your victories without letting external standards overshadow your accomplishments. Find happiness in your individual journey, free from the constraints of comparison.

Mind Games: Decoding the Psychology of Comparison

You may be constantly evaluating yourself and others in various areas like attractiveness, wealth, intelligence, and success. It's estimated that up to 10% of your thoughts involve comparing yourself to others in some way (Social Comparison Theory, 2019). Social comparison theory suggests that you gauge your social and personal worth by measuring how you compare to those around you. Psychologist Leon Festinger first developed this theory in 1954, and subsequent research has supported its validity.

When you regularly compare yourself to others, it becomes motivation to strive for improvement. However, it can also trigger negative emotions such as dissatisfaction regret, or remorse. In some cases, constant comparison may even trigger destructive behaviors such as lying or engaging in disordered eating habits. It's essential to be mindful of how much you compare yourself to others and how it affects your mental and emotional well-being. Striving for self-improvement is admirable, but it's equally important to cultivate self-compassion and focus on your own journey rather than constantly measuring yourself against others.

According to this theory, you continually evaluate yourself by measuring your abilities, achievements, and attributes against those of others in your social environment. This theory comprises three main concepts of social comparisons:

- **Upward social comparison**

Comparing yourself to those you admire can frequently leave you feeling inadequate or driven to get better. For example, you might compare your career achievements to a colleague who has reached a higher professional position, this leads to aspirations for personal growth.

- **Downward social comparison**

It involves assessing yourself in relation to individuals whom you perceive as less successful or competent. This type of comparison tends to boost self-esteem and can provide a sense of satisfaction or gratitude for your own situation. For instance, if you compare your fitness level to someone who is less physically active, you may feel a sense of accomplishment.

- **Lateral social comparison**

This one happens when you compare yourself to people who are at a similar level in a certain area of your life. This comparison can be used as a standard by which to evaluate your growth or proficiency within a peer group. For example, comparing your academic performance to that of your classmates can encourage you to put in more effort or continue at your current level of excellence.

Seeing carefully crafted online images all the time can make you compare yourself to others, which can make you feel bad about yourself. On social media, people usually show only the best parts of their lives, like cool vacations or big achievements. But when you see these posts, you might start thinking your own life doesn't measure up.

For example, imagine you're on Instagram, and all your friends are posting amazing pictures. It's easy to start feeling like your own life isn't as exciting or perfect as theirs. This can make you feel like you're not good enough. The same thing can happen when you see people on LinkedIn showing off their big accomplishments; it might make you feel like you're not successful enough.

Celebrities and influencers make this even worse by showing off their glamorous lives, making you feel like you should be just like them. And when you start measuring your worth by things like how many likes or followers you have, it can really mess with your head.

What you see online isn't always real life. It's important to be true to yourself and not compare yourself to others too much. Being authentic online is more important than trying to be perfect, and it's okay if your life isn't as flashy as it seems on social media.

The Role of Social Media

Social media has a big impact on how teenagers compare themselves to others. When you're on social media, you see lots of pictures and posts that make people's lives look perfect. It can make you feel like your own life doesn't measure up. You might start feeling bad about yourself because you're comparing yourself to what you see online. The more likes and followers someone gets, the more popular and accepted they feel. This can make you feel like you need to measure your own worth based on how many likes or followers you have.

Also, there's FOMO (Fear of Missing Out) where you worry about not doing as much fun stuff as other people. You see all the cool things others are doing online, and it makes you feel like you're missing out. This can make you feel anxious and unhappy.

Sometimes, people on social media can be mean because they can hide behind their screens. They might say hurtful things or bully others online. This makes things even worse for teenagers' mental health. So, while social media can be fun, it's important to be careful and not let it make you feel bad about yourself.

Social Comparison Bias

When you consistently deviate from rationality in judgment and base your conclusions more on feelings than on factual information, this is known as *cognitive bias*. These biases often stem from mental shortcuts or heuristics that the brain uses to simplify complex information processing tasks. They can influence your perception, memory, and decision-making, which leads to skewed interpretations of reality.

Social comparison involves evaluating yourself in relation to others, and this often leads to feelings of superiority or inferiority. These comparisons might be distorted by cognitive biases that emphasize data that confirms preconceived notions or prejudices, such as the availability heuristic or confirmation bias. For example, if you constantly compare yourself to highly curated social media profiles, you may develop an unrealistic perception of your own life and abilities, and this may lead to feelings of inadequacy.

This link between cognitive bias and social comparison can significantly impact self-esteem. Constant exposure to biased information and unrealistic standards can exacerbate feelings of insecurity and self-doubt. Also, confirmation bias may lead you to seek out information that confirms negative self-perceptions, further eroding self-esteem.

Shattered Self: How Constant Comparison Impacts Mental Health

This constant comparison affects our mental health in many different ways, and they include:

- **Negative Self-Evaluation**

You put yourself through a vicious cycle of self-evaluation when you compare yourself to other people all the time. Your mental health and self-esteem suffer when you measure your worth in proportion to other people's expectations, which makes you feel inadequate. Continuous comparison can cause you to concentrate on your perceived shortcomings, which can undermine your confidence and breed self-doubt. This behavior frequently ignores one's own accomplishments and strengths, which distorts one's perception of oneself. Increased tension, anxiety, and self-doubt can result from the unrelenting pursuit of unachievable goals. Realizing that each person's journey is unique and that comparing oneself to others only impedes personal development is crucial. The pattern can be broken by embracing self-acceptance and celebrating your unique successes. This will improve your relationship with yourself and enhance your mental health.

- **Anxiety and Depression**

The rise in social isolation among young adults is closely tied to escalating depression and anxiety levels. As social media engagement increases, many experience high social isolation due to constant exposure to meticulously curated and unrealistic depictions of others' lives. A 2016 observational study found that young adults spending more time on social media had a 15–20% higher likelihood of depression. Also, those using seven or more platforms were three times more likely to face increased depression and anxiety (Osorio & Hyde, 2021).

This has led to a high comparison rate, which has eventually led to high levels of anxiety and depression among teenagers. Constant exposure to idealized images and lifestyles on social media platforms can lead unrealistic expectations and feelings of inadequacy. As you compare yourself to others, you may perceive yourself as falling short or not measuring up, leading to a sense of low self-esteem and self-worth. Also, when you continuously try to keep up with others, FOMO (fear of missing out) can intensify feelings of worry and loneliness. This constant comparing might set off a chain reaction of unfavorable ideas and feelings that raises anxiety and depressive symptoms. For that reason, recognizing the influence of comparison culture and actively managing your exposure to comparison triggers is essential for maintaining positive mental health.

- **Body Image Concerns**

When you constantly compare yourself to others, especially on social media where images are often curated to perfection, it can significantly impact how you perceive your own body. This comparison can lead to body image dissatisfaction, where you may feel insecure or unhappy with your appearance because you don't match up to the seemingly flawless images you see online.

You may feel under pressure to meet unattainable beauty standards as you get around through social media feeds that are replete with filtered and photoshopped photos. These standards, often perpetuated by influencers and celebrities, can create a sense of inadequacy as you strive to achieve an idealized version of beauty that may not be realistic or attainable. Amidst the overwhelming pressure to conform to unrealistic beauty standards on social media, you may experience self-doubt and low self-esteem. It's crucial to acknowledge that online representations often deviate from reality. Instead of comparing yourself to these unattainable standards, prioritize self-acceptance and self-love, embracing your authentic self.

Empowering Growth: Strategies to Defeat the Comparison Culture

Cultivating Self-Awareness

Self-awareness is understanding yourself, including your thoughts, feelings, behaviors, and motivations. It means being conscious of your strengths, weaknesses, values, and beliefs. When you're self-aware, you recognize your emotions as they arise and understand why you feel a certain way. You're also aware of how your actions and words impact yourself and others. Self-awareness involves reflecting on your experiences, choices, and reactions, allowing you to gain insights into your personality and identity.

The importance of self-awareness to teens lies in its role in personal growth and development. When teens are self-aware, they can make better decisions, set realistic goals, and navigate challenges more effectively. It gives them the confidence to pinpoint their areas of weakness and take proactive measures to better themselves. In addition, as self-aware teens are better able to express their needs and boundaries and empathize with others' perspectives, they also build healthier connections.

Strategies for Cultivating Self-Awareness and Challenging Comparison

To encourage and develop self-awareness, you can follow the following tips:

- **Encourage open discussion of challenges with your child:**

You play a big part in making your child feel okay about talking about their problems. Tell them it's good to share how they feel and what's bothering them. They need to understand that it's okay to make mistakes because that's just part of growing up. Talking about tough stuff is important for getting better and learning. When you show you're there for them and that you're open to talking, they feel safe dealing with their problems.

- **Point out the positives:**

As a parent, your role involves actively recognizing and appreciating your child's unique strengths and accomplishments. Train yourself to be attentive to their efforts, big or small. Remind them of their successes, reinforcing a positive mindset that extends beyond comparing themselves to others. By highlighting their achievements, you contribute to building their self-esteem and resilience.

- **Foster a balanced perspective:**

You have the opportunity to shape your child's outlook on life by helping them embrace individuality. Guide them in understanding that each person possesses distinctive qualities, and life isn't a perpetual competition. Encourage them to value differences and emphasize that success manifests in various forms. Through your guidance, they learn to appreciate diversity and recognize that comparing themselves to others is not the measure of true success.

- **Discourage comparisons:**

Remind yourself that everyone has their unique path in life. When you catch yourself comparing, consider the diverse journeys people undertake. Focus on your individual progress, acknowledging that growth and success are personal and don't need validation through constant comparison. Embrace the idea that your journey is distinct, and so is everyone else's.

- **Encourage your child to be a member of the team:**

It's important to understand that when working together as a team, individuals can often achieve more than they do when working alone. Encourage your child to join in group activities and work with others. Let them know that being part of a team gives them a feeling of belonging and that everyone's efforts count towards reaching goals together. It's like being part of a big team where everyone helps each other out and celebrates successes together. So, remind your child to be an active part of the team and enjoy the journey of achieving things together with others.

- **Don't always gloss over mistakes:**

You should know that everyone messes up sometimes, including you. Tell your child that making mistakes is actually a good thing because they help us learn. Instead of avoiding talking about mistakes, it's better to have open conversations about them. Let your child know that it's totally normal to make mistakes and that it's part of growing up. Help them see that when we face challenges and learn from our mistakes, we become better and stronger. By sharing your own stories of mistakes and what you learned from them, you show your child that learning from mistakes is something we do throughout our lives to become better people.

- **Provide opportunities for independence:**

Help your kid learn how to make choices and be responsible for them. Tell them that being able to do things on their own is really important for growing up. When you let them decide things, it makes them feel strong and capable. Let them pick what they like and make their own decisions. This helps them feel more sure of themselves and understand who they are. They won't need to look to others to know if they're doing okay. When you give them room to try things out, it helps them feel good about themselves.

- **Journaling:**

You can suggest to your child to start their own personal journal where they can write about their experiences and feelings. Tell them that journaling is like a way to explore themselves and learn more about who they are. Explain that writing down their thoughts can be really helpful and comforting. It's like talking to a close friend who understands everything without judging. By keeping a journal, they can understand themselves better and appreciate what makes them special.

Promoting Authenticity

Authenticity involves being true to yourself, acknowledging strengths and vulnerabilities, while self-acceptance involves embracing your unique qualities without undue comparison to others. Recognizing and celebrating individuality can break the chains of constant comparison, which leads to a healthier mindset and promotes genuine self-worth.

You can follow the following tips if you want to live an authentic life.

- **Providing a safe space:**

Create a place where you feel safe to be yourself. It's important that you know your thoughts, feelings, and who you are. This way, you can be completely honest without being afraid of what others might think. It's all about feeling truly secure and accepted, which helps you feel safe and comfortable.

- **Affirming conversations:**

Actively participate in conversations that not only acknowledge but celebrate your unique qualities. In these dialogues, it's important that you feel genuinely heard and understood. Engaging in affirming conversations reinforces the idea that you are appreciated for being exactly who you are, and your individuality is respected.

- **Encouraging self-expression:**

Take advantage of opportunities to express yourself through various channels such as art, writing, or any form of creativity. Grant yourself the freedom to communicate your thoughts and feelings authentically. By embracing diverse means of self-expression, you empower yourself to share your uniqueness confidently.

- **Encouraging authenticity of identity:**

Remember, you should embrace who you are without reservations. It's perfectly acceptable to explore and fully accept your identity. By doing so, you foster a sense of authenticity that not only brings you a profound sense of fulfillment but also strengthens your connections with yourself and those around you. Encouraging your authentic self allows for genuine and meaningful interactions, forming a deeper understanding of your unique qualities.

- **Celebrating milestones of independence and authenticity:**

As you navigate through life, take the time to acknowledge and celebrate those moments when you assert your independence and fully embrace your authentic self. Consider these milestones as pivotal achievements in your personal journey. By recognizing and celebrating these steps, you reinforce the significance of staying true to yourself. Each instance of embracing independence and authenticity is a triumph, contributing to your growth and shaping a more genuine and fulfilling life.

Fostering Gratitude

Making gratitude a habit can help you fight against feeling bad when you're always comparing yourself to others. When you focus on what you're thankful for, you take away the power of comparing yourself to others. It's like shifting your attention from what you don't have to appreciating what you do have. Being thankful makes you feel better about yourself, boosts your confidence, and makes you see the good things around you.

When you recognize the good things in your life, it makes you mentally stronger and stops you from feeling bad due to always comparing yourself to others. Being thankful helps you stay in the present moment and see things in a more positive way instead of always thinking about what others have that you don't. It's like a tool that changes your perspective, making you focus on being happy and feeling good about yourself instead of comparing yourself to others all the time.

Benefits of Gratitude for Teens

Gratitude holds numerous benefits for teenagers, positively impacting various aspects of their lives:

- **Improved sleep:**

Taking a moment to feel thankful before going to bed can actually help you sleep better. When you think about good things that happened during your day and appreciate the stuff you have, it can make you feel less stressed and worried. And when you're less stressed, it's easier to drift off into a peaceful sleep. Getting enough sleep is really important for your body, mind, and how well you think. It helps you stay healthy, feel good emotionally, and think clearly. So, when you wake up in the morning after a good night's sleep, you're ready to tackle whatever comes your way.

- **Reduced suicide risk:**

Being thankful can help teens stay safe from thoughts of hurting themselves or feeling really hopeless. When teens are grateful, they start to see how good life can be and how important it is to them. Instead of feeling down, they focus on the good things happening in their life. This helps them feel more hopeful and less like hurting themselves or thinking about suicide.

- **Increased social connection:**

Feeling thankful and showing it brings teens closer to their friends. When they say "thank you" or do something nice for others, like helping out or giving compliments, it brings them closer together and makes them trust each other more. This feeling of being close helps them feel like they belong and are accepted. When teens feel connected to their friends and community, they feel happier and stronger, even when things get tough.

- **Improved mood:**

Expressing gratitude can really make a big difference in how teens feel. When you think about the good things in your life, it helps you see things in a more positive way and feel happier. It's like a natural mood booster that brings feelings of joy and satisfaction. When teens make a habit of being thankful, it helps them handle tough times better and stay positive even when things get hard.

Interactive Element

Gratitude Journal

If you want your teen to feel happier and have a better mental attitude, suggesting they start a gratitude journal can really help. It's an easy thing to do, but it can make a big difference in how they see the world.

Daily Reflections for Your Gratitude Journal:

Each day, encourage them to take a moment to sit down with their journal. Remind them that it is a time for self-reflection and appreciation. Here are some prompts to help them reflect and get started:

- Share the positive highlight of your day by describing the most uplifting moment.

- Identify and list five small elements in your daily life that provide consistent support.

- Jot down three things at this very moment that evoke a sense of gratitude.

- Despite facing challenges, find and note three things you remain grateful for.

- Express appreciation for five items you use regularly in your daily life.

- Identify the person you would turn to in an emergency situation.

- Take a moment to write a note of thanks to yourself.

To conclude, the pervasive culture of comparison, amplified by social media and societal pressures, significantly impacts teenagers' mental health. Constant evaluation against others leads to negative self-evaluation, anxiety, depression, and body image concerns. It's crucial to foster self-awareness, encouraging teens to embrace their unique journey, avoid comparisons, and celebrate individuality. Authenticity, gratitude practices, and parental support are powerful tools in mitigating the harmful effects of comparison culture. By promoting these strategies, we empower teens to build resilience, navigate challenges, and foster a positive mindset for their overall well-being. Reflect on your experiences, break free from comparison, and join the journey towards healthier mental states.

In the next chapter, you will gain a comprehensive understanding of body dysmorphia in teenagers.

Unveiling Self-Image: Confronting Body Dysmorphia

No amount of self-improvement can make up for any lack of self-acceptance. –Robert Holden

You, as an individual, must recognize that self-acceptance is not a replaceable trait. Despite efforts towards self-improvement, genuine contentment comes from acknowledging and accepting your true self. No external improvements can compensate for the impact of self-acceptance on your mental health. When you are dealing with body dysmorphia, you should understand and appreciate your self-worth.

Mirror Reflections: Understanding Negative Body Image

Body Dysmorphic Disorder (BDD) is where a teen may worry too much about perceived imperfections in their appearance. When they have BDDS, the teen tends to have some repetitive behaviors like checking, fixing, or concealing certain body parts. Unlike normal insecurities, those with

BDD put a lot of focus on minute imperfections, invisible to others. This causes distress and affects daily life.

You might notice your teenager spending a lot of time looking at themselves in the mirror, thinking even small imperfections make them less valuable. They might stay away from others because they feel like people are judging them. This can make them feel really sad and alone. Being so focused on their appearance can make it hard for them to hang out with friends, which can lead them to feel down and not do so well overall.

Some teens experience constantly seeking reassurance about their appearance or avoiding social events due to an overwhelming fear of judgment. For instance, a girl may spend hours trying to perfect her makeup, convinced it will conceal an imagined flaw.

The Psychological Impact

BDD and School

Having Body Dysmorphic Disorder (BDD) can really mess with how well you do in school. When you're constantly worried about how you look, it's super hard to focus on your studies. This means you might not do so great on tests and assignments.

BDD also messes with your social life at school. You end up feeling really self-conscious and anxious around other people, which can make you want to avoid being around them altogether. Sometimes, BDD can get so bad that you don't even want to go to school anymore, or you end up dropping out.

Moving from one grade to another can make BDD even worse. It's like starting over in a new place but feeling even more anxious about how you look. This can make you do things over and over again to try to feel better about yourself, which just makes everything harder. So, having BDD can make school really tough, but it's important to know that there's help out there to make things better.

Social Media and BDD

Different types of bullying, like making fun of someone's body, whether it's online or in person, can really hurt how you see yourself and make you feel bad about who you are. Especially during teenage years when you're already dealing with a lot of pressure from society, being bullied about your body can make things even tougher. Body shaming is when people tease or criticize how you look, focusing on things like your weight, size, or your personal relationship habits.

This kind of bullying often makes children feel like they want to stay away from others because they're afraid of being judged. Studies have shown that a lot of young people who struggle with feeling embarrassed or ashamed about how they look end up feeling really isolated and unhappy.

Social media doesn't directly cause these feelings, but it can make them worse, especially for teenagers who are already struggling with how they see themselves. Seeing all those perfect-looking people on social media can make you feel like you're not good enough. It's like you're always comparing yourself to these unrealistic standards of beauty, which can make you feel even worse about yourself. This can be especially tough for those who are already vulnerable to feeling bad about their bodies.

Recognizing Symptoms

If you see the following behavior in a teenager, it's really important to talk to them kindly and try to understand what they're going through. With the right help and support, teenagers can learn how to deal with their feelings better and feel happier overall.

- **Focus on their looks to an extreme**

Teenagers who struggle with body dysmorphia often become trapped in a never-ending worry about how they look. It goes beyond just normal concerns about appearance and becomes something they can't stop thinking about. For example, they might spend hours staring at themselves in the mirror, picking apart every little thing they don't like. They might even develop habits like constantly measuring or touching the parts of their body they're unhappy with, hoping it'll make them feel better.

This obsession can get so intense that it starts to interfere with their everyday life. It might make it hard for them to focus in school or to hang out with friends like they used to.

These teenagers might also constantly ask for reassurance from people around them, like friends or family, about how they look. They're always seeking compliments or approval to make themselves feel better, even if it's just for a little while. This constant need for other people to say nice things about them can strain relationships and make them feel even more alone because others might not understand just how much they're struggling with their appearance.

- **Feel upset about their appearance**

Imagine feeling really unhappy about how you look to the point where it's all you can think about. That's what teenagers with body dysmorphia go through. They see themselves in a distorted way, thinking they have flaws that are much worse than they really are. It's like looking in a funhouse mirror that makes you look all weird and distorted.

Being around other people can be tough for them because they feel like everyone is judging them. They might avoid going out with friends because they're scared of being made fun of. Even simple things like getting dressed or putting on makeup can make them feel super anxious and unsure of themselves.

These feelings of unhappiness can take over their whole life, making them feel worthless and stealing away the fun of being a teenager. Sometimes, it gets so bad that they might hurt themselves or even think about ending their life because they can't stand feeling so bad about themselves all the time.

- **Check or fix their body parts often**

It's pretty common for teenagers with body dysmorphia to constantly check or try to "fix" what they see as flaws in their appearance. This could mean they spend a lot of time looking in the mirror, touching their skin, or trying to hide certain body parts. These actions are like rituals they feel they have to do to feel better about how they look, even though their view of themselves is distorted.

For example, a girl with body dysmorphia might spend ages looking at her skin, trying to make it perfect by touching or picking at it. Or a boy might spend hours fixing his hair, hoping it'll hide what he sees as a problem with his hairline.

Sometimes, teens with body dysmorphia go to extremes to hide how they feel about their appearance. They might wear a lot of makeup or clothes that cover them up completely, no matter if it's hot or cold outside. They might also avoid situations where they think people will notice how they look, like going swimming or to a party where there might be pictures taken. These behaviors help them cope with feeling upset about how they see themselves.

- **Try not to be seen**

Some teenagers who struggle with body dysmorphia really don't like being seen or having their picture taken, especially in situations where they feel exposed or vulnerable. They might skip parties, school events, or anything where people might look closely at how they look. This fear comes from worrying that others will judge or reject them because of what they see as flaws in their appearance.

For instance, a teenager dealing with body dysmorphia might say "no" to going to a pool party or the beach because they're scared others will notice and say mean things about their body shape or size. They might also avoid joining sports teams or activities where they have to wear tight clothes, because they're scared of people comparing them to others and saying bad stuff. In really tough situations, they might even stay home from school to avoid being around their classmates.

They might also be super careful about what they share online, making sure only to post pictures where they look good. They might avoid showing their whole body or use editing tools to change how they look before putting pictures online. Being so worried about what others think can make them feel really lonely and separate from everyone else.

- **Have false ideas about their looks**

Sometimes, teenagers with body dysmorphia see themselves in a way that's not true. They might think something is wrong with how they look, even if others tell them it's not true. For example, they might believe their nose is too big or their skin has lots of scars, even if it's not really like that. This can make them avoid being around others or stop doing things they enjoy because they're worried about how they look. They might spend a lot of time trying to fix what they see as flaws, like spending hours on skincare or even wanting to get surgery. Even if people try to show them the truth, they might still believe their thoughts. This can make them feel really upset and make it hard for them to do normal stuff in their lives.

The Influence of Digital Platforms on Body Image and Self-Perception

Positive Effects

- **Body positivity:**

Body positivity is about feeling good about yourself and accepting your body just the way it is. Especially on social media, it's all about showing real pictures of all kinds of bodies. In a good online space, people share pictures of themselves without editing or changing how they look. They want to show that all bodies are beautiful, no matter their shape, size, color, abilities, or gender. The idea is to challenge the old ideas of what's considered beautiful and create a space where everyone feels included and happy with who they are. Body-positive posts are not about showing off or making things look perfect. Instead, they're about celebrating the uniqueness of every body and showing that there's beauty in being different.

- **Health and fitness inspiration:**

Social media can actually help teenagers stay healthy and active. You'll find lots of accounts on apps like Instagram and TikTok that are all about showing cool stuff related to staying fit and eating right. They share things like workout tips, yummy recipes, and ideas for living healthier. The goal is to encourage teens to take good care of themselves and make healthy choices. These accounts want to show that being healthy is totally doable and can be fun too! By sharing all this positive stuff about being healthy, they're helping to make sure more teens care about their bodies and want to be healthy overall.

- **Community and support:**

For teens dealing with body image issues or feeling down about themselves, social media can actually be a helpful place to find support and friends. There are lots of groups online where people who are going through similar stuff can connect and chat. Being part of these groups can make you feel like you're not alone and that there are others who get what you're going through. It's like having a bunch of friends who understand and cheer you on. Being part of these online communities can really boost your confidence and help you feel better about yourself. It's like having a support system that's always there for you, which can make a big difference when you're struggling with how you feel about your body.

Negative Effects

Negative effects of social media on body image are particularly pertinent to teenagers, who are at a vulnerable stage of development where self-perception and identity are heavily influenced by external factors. Let's break down each aspect:

- **Unrealistic beauty standards**:

You see a lot of perfect-looking people on social media, but most of those pictures are changed a lot to look that way. For teens who are still figuring out who they are, seeing these images can make them feel like they're not good enough. It can make them feel bad about how they look because they think they have to be just like those edited pictures, which isn't realistic.

- **Comparison and competition**:

Being a teenager means you're really aware of yourself and always comparing yourself to others. Social media makes this even more intense because you're always seeing pictures of people looking perfect. It's easy to start comparing your body to theirs and feeling like you're not good enough. This can make you feel bad about yourself and not see yourself clearly.

- **Cyberbullying**:

Because social media lets people hide their identity, cyberbullying has become a big problem for teens. Mean comments about how you look can really hurt, especially since they can spread quickly and stay online forever. Cyberbullying can make you feel really bad about yourself and make any worries you already have about how you look even worse.

- **Worsening of body-image disorders**:

Teens who already struggle with how they see their bodies, like those with body dysmorphic disorder (BDD), can find social media really tough. Seeing perfect-looking people all the time can make their feelings even worse, making them obsess over their appearance and avoid being around others.

Lots of teens compare themselves to others on social media, which can make body issues worse. Seeing all those perfect photos and lives can make them feel like they're not good enough. But you can help your teens deal with this. By teaching them to think critically about what they see online and talking openly about how social media isn't real life, you can make it easier for them to handle these feelings.

- **Talk about media literacy:**

Media literacy means helping teens learn how to look at things online and figure out if they're true or if they're trying to trick you. You can teach teens to be careful and not believe everything they see on social media. By showing them how to think critically and question what they see, teens can get better at telling what's real and what's just for show. This helps them not feel bad about themselves when they compare themselves to what they see online.

- **Be a positive role model:**

You play a big part in how teenagers think about their bodies. If you show them how to use social media in a healthy way and act positively about your own body, they'll likely do the same. Being okay with who you are, focusing on what makes you unique, and not saying bad things about yourself can make your home a happier place. This helps balance out the bad stuff they might see on social media, where people often compare themselves to others and feel bad about how they look.

- **Monitor social media use:**

It's important to keep an eye on what your teens are doing on social media and talk to them about it. By knowing what they see online, you can spot anything that might be bad for them and deal with it before it becomes a problem. Make sure they feel okay talking to you about what they do online so you can help them if they need it. This way, you can make sure they have a good experience on social media and stay safe.

- **Encourage positive self-talk:**

Encouraging positive self-talk means helping teens develop a good way of thinking about themselves. You can show them how to question negative thoughts they have about their bodies and focus on accepting themselves. It's about recognizing what makes them special and reminding them of their strengths and successes. This way, they won't feel so bad when they compare themselves to others on social media. By doing this, you can boost their confidence and make them feel better overall.

Filtering Reality

Social media sites like Instagram and TikTok are places where famous people, called influencers, often show off what they think is beautiful. They use fancy tricks like filters and editing tools to change how they look in pictures and videos. This makes them seem perfect, but it's not real. When teenagers see these images all the time, they might feel bad about themselves because they think they don't look as good. It can make them feel like they're not good enough or like their body isn't right. Seeing these fake pictures all the time can make teenagers think they need to look like that too, even though it's not possible.

You can discern reality from digitally altered images for your child by following these tips:

- Help your teen see that what makes a person valuable goes way beyond just looks. Talk to them about qualities like kindness, intelligence, creativity, and empathy. These are the things that really matter. By showing them that there's more to beauty than what's on the outside, they'll develop a healthier view of themselves and others.

- Remind your teen that beauty is different for everyone. Everyone's idea of what's beautiful is unique, and that's a good thing! Encourage them to appreciate diversity and understand that there's no one "right" way to look. When they see beauty as something personal, they'll be more accepting of themselves and others.

- Teach your teen to be smart about what they see online. Help them think critically about the stuff they come across on social media. Are those pictures real, or have they been changed? Encourage them to follow accounts that celebrate realness and diversity instead of ones that push impossible beauty standards.

- Encourage your teenager to do more than just scroll through social media. Get them to share their own stuff, talk to others, and be part of the conversation. By being active online, they can show who they really are and not just follow what others say is cool.

Beyond the Surface: Cultivating Confidence and Self-Worth

Strength in Diversity

Apart from how they look on the outside, teenagers should learn to appreciate and be proud of their inner strengths and abilities. This means recognizing and celebrating the things that make them unique and special, like their personality, kindness, ability to bounce back from tough times, and their creativity. By focusing on these inner qualities, teens can understand that their worth goes way beyond just how they look. When they learn to value these inner traits, it builds a strong foundation for feeling good about themselves and being able to handle whatever life throws at them. This approach helps teens develop genuine confidence by showing them that they're awesome just the way they are. Ultimately, when teens learn to treasure and embrace their inner qualities, it boosts their self-esteem and makes them better equipped to deal with criticism or negativity from others.

Creating Safe Spaces

This emphasizes the importance of creating spaces where teenagers can openly share their body image concerns and seek support without the fear of being judged. Building a safe and supportive environment involves promoting understanding, empathy, and acceptance. These teenagers can gain several benefits from these safe spaces. To begin to create them:

- **Start the conversation early:**

Encouraging discussions about body image from an early age emphasizes the significance of addressing these concerns proactively. When you initiate conversations at a young age, it becomes easy for them to develop a healthy mindset and open communication channel. This allows them to express themselves and seek guidance when needed.

- **Encourage healthy habits:**

Getting teenagers to make good choices like exercising often, eating healthy, and getting enough sleep helps them feel good about themselves in every way.

- **Focus on health, not appearance:**

Shifting the focus from appearance to health is crucial in promoting a positive body image. This approach encourages teens to value their bodies for their functionality and health rather than conforming to societal beauty standards. It helps create a mindset that prioritizes health over unrealistic physical ideals.

- **Focusing on the whole person:**

Encouraging a holistic perspective means looking at people in a complete way. It's about understanding that how someone looks is only one part of who they are. Having a positive self-image means appreciating all the different parts that make someone unique and special. It's about recognizing that there's more to someone than just their appearance. So, when we encourage this way of thinking, we help people feel good about themselves by valuing everything that makes them who they are.

- **Listen and validate their feelings:**

Actively listening to teenagers and validating their feelings is key to creating a supportive environment. It involves acknowledging their concerns, emotions, and experiences without judgment. Providing a space where they feel heard and understood fosters trust and encourages them to open up about their body image struggles.

- **Be mindful of language:**

Language shapes perceptions. Being mindful of the words used when discussing body image is essential to avoid reinforcing harmful stereotypes or unrealistic ideals.

Choosing language that promotes positivity, acceptance, and encouragement contributes to creating a safe and supportive atmosphere for discussing body image concerns.

Building Resilience

To aid teenagers to develop resilience and coping skills, especially when facing societal pressures and grappling with body dysmorphia, consider introducing them to a range of practical tools and resources:

- **Mindfulness meditation:**

You can help your child try out mindfulness meditation. There are many ways to do it, such as:

  - **Mindful meditation:** It's a way of paying attention to what's happening right now without judging it. This can be really helpful for reducing stress and feeling better about themselves.

  - **Mindful exercise:** Introduce the concept of incorporating mindfulness into physical activity. It means paying attention and being in the moment while you're exercising. Instead of just going through the motions, really focus on how your body feels and what you're doing. This helps you connect your mind and body, making your workouts more effective and enjoyable. So, next time you're exercising, try to be present and really tune in to what you're doing; you might find it makes a big difference!

○ **Mindful eating:** Promote mindful eating habits by encouraging teenagers to savor and appreciate each bite. This practice can help develop a healthier relationship with food and reduce stress related to body image.

○ **Mindful coloring and drawing:** Suggest engaging in mindful activities such as coloring or drawing. These creative outlets provide a space for self-expression and relaxation, offering a break from societal pressures.

- **Avoiding triggers:**

Encourage teenagers to identify and steer clear of triggers that may negatively impact their body image. This could involve recognizing specific social media accounts, situations, or conversations that contribute to feelings of inadequacy and actively avoiding them.

- **Avoiding comparisons:**

Emphasize the importance of avoiding constant comparisons with others. Remind teenagers that everyone's journey is unique, and comparing themselves to others can lead to unrealistic standards and unnecessary stress.

- **Limiting time spent on appearance:**

Encourage teenagers to cut back on routines that focus too much on appearance, which can make you feel bad about your body. Instead, try to accept yourself for who you are, and don't spend too much time on grooming or habits related to how you look.

- **Art and music therapy:**

Introduce the therapeutic benefits of art and music. Art therapy is when you use painting, drawing, or other creative stuff to express how you feel inside. It's like talking without using words. When you do art, it helps you let out your emotions and thoughts in a cool way.

Then there's music therapy, which is like using music to make you feel good. Music can be super comforting and make you feel happy or inspired. Sometimes, when you're feeling down, listening to your favorite song can really lift your spirits up. So, both art and music can be like friends that help you feel better when you're going through tough times.

Promoting Self-Compassion

Treating yourself kindly, understanding your own feelings, and accepting yourself, especially when things are tough, is what self-compassion is all about. This is super important for teens because it helps them build a good relationship with themselves, making them feel better emotionally and stronger when facing challenges.

Teenage years can be tough with school stress, peer pressure, and figuring out who you are. Self-compassion makes it easier to deal with all that by helping teens understand themselves better and not being too hard on themselves when things don't go well. Instead of beating themselves up over mistakes, they learn to be as nice to themselves as they would to a friend, which boosts their confidence and helps them stay emotionally steady.

Plus, self-compassion helps teens deal with pressure from society to be perfect. It teaches them to accept that everyone makes mistakes and that it's okay not to be perfect. This makes it easier for them to handle criticism and feel connected to others. In the end, self-compassion gives teens the tools they need to handle the ups and downs of being a teenager with more strength and a better opinion of themselves.

Strategies for Promoting Self-Compassion Practices Among Teenagers

First, build a relationship that helps your teenage child feel secure and nurtures self-compassion in many ways:

- Spending time with your child is super important! Doing fun stuff together helps you both feel closer and happier. Just being there for them and doing things they enjoy shows them how much you care.

- Listening carefully when your child talks is key. It shows them that you care about what they think and feel. And when you listen without judging or interrupting, they feel safe opening up to you and sharing their thoughts.

- Everyone makes mistakes, including kids. Forgiving your child when they mess up shows them that you love them no matter what. It creates a loving atmosphere where they feel comfortable being themselves.

- Being kind to each other in the family is really nice. Small acts of kindness, like helping out or saying "thank you," make everyone feel good and loved. It's like spreading happiness around your home!

- When your child does something great, make sure to praise them! Letting them know you're proud of them boosts their confidence and makes them feel good about themselves. It shows them that their efforts matter and encourages them to keep doing their best.

Then, you can also encourage and build self-compassion in your teenagers. You can implement the following tips to do it effectively:

- Tell your child it's good to stop for a moment and think about how they're feeling. By paying attention to their emotions, they can understand them better and learn how to handle them.

- Tell your child that everyone faces tough times and that's normal. It's okay to have difficulties and make mistakes. And it's totally fine to ask for help when they need it.

- Teach your child to be nice to themselves by saying positive things. When they talk to themselves with kindness, it helps them feel good about who they are and become stronger inside.

Interactive Element

You can help the teens in your care develop a positive body image through reflective journaling. Here are 20 prompts to guide their introspection and encourage deeper reflection:

1. Reflect on a time when your body made you feel proud and strong.

2. Write about a compliment you received that made you appreciate your body.

3. Describe a physical feature you admire in yourself and why.

4. Explore how your body has helped you accomplish a personal goal or overcome a challenge.

5. Consider how societal standards of beauty have influenced your perception of yourself.

6. List three things you love about your body, regardless of what others may think.

7. Reflect on a moment when you felt comfortable and confident in your own skin.

8. Write about a role model who embraces diverse body types and inspires you to do the same.

9. Consider how your attitude towards your body impacts your overall well-being.

10. Describe an activity or hobby that brings you joy and makes you feel connected to your body.

11. Reflect on how you talk to yourself about your body and consider if it's supportive or critical.

12. Explore how media representations of beauty have affected your self-image.

13. Describe a time when you felt pressure to conform to unrealistic beauty standards and how you handled it.

14. Reflect on a moment when you realized that your worth isn't tied to your appearance.

15. Write about a physical activity that makes you feel strong and empowered.

16. Consider how your body image affects your relationships with others and yourself.

17. Describe a time when you compared yourself to others and how it made you feel.

18. Reflect on a body-positive affirmation that resonates with you and why.

19. Write about a future goal that isn't related to your appearance, focusing on personal growth and fulfillment.

Encourage teens to use these prompts as opportunities for self-discovery, understanding, and appreciation of their bodies, which leads to a healthier and more positive body image.

In conclusion, recognizing the significance of self-acceptance, independent of external improvements, is crucial. BDD impacts teens, leading to obsessive behaviors and social withdrawal. Social media exacerbates these issues by promoting unrealistic beauty standards and facilitating cyberbullying. However, positive aspects, like body positivity and community support, can counteract these negative influences. Recognizing symptoms, promoting media literacy, and encouraging healthy habits are practical strategies. Creating safe spaces for open discussions and fostering resilience through self-compassion practices are equally important. By implementing these measures, we can provide teenagers with the support they need to navigate body image struggles and promote their overall well-being.

In the next chapter, you will gain a comprehensive understanding of eating disorders in teenagers, equipped with the knowledge to recognize warning signs, initiate early intervention, and provide effective support, fostering healing and empowerment in teenagers struggling with disordered eating behaviors.

Make a Difference with Your Review

Unlock the Power of Generosity

Parenting in the digital age is tough. My book, "Teen Mental Health," offers guidance on how to support your child's emotional wellbeing amid online challenges.

Could you help other parents by sharing your thoughts on this book? Your review can provide crucial support to someone just like you.

Please take a moment to leave a review.

It's free, quick, and could help another family:

Simply scan the QR code below and share your experience:

Thank you for your generosity and support.

- Heidi R. Crow

Eating Disorders: Healing the Relationship With Food

I won't let a number on a scale own me. –Unknown

Understanding the Complexity of Eating Disorders

When we talk of eating disorders, we mean conditions that lead to changes in how a person eats and thinks about food, as well as their emotions and perceptions related to their body. These disorders can lead to significant harm to their physical health and, at the same time, influence their mental health. These eating disorders come in different forms, which include:

- **Overeating:**

This occurs when someone eats more food than their body needs. And it is not just about regular meals; you might find someone eating large amounts of food quickly, often to the point of feeling uncomfortably full. An example of this could be eating an entire bag of chips in one sitting, even if not hungry.

- **Undereating:**

This is the opposite of overeating. Undereating happens when a person consistently eats insufficient amounts of food, not meeting their body's nutritional needs. It often involves restrictive eating patterns and can lead to malnutrition and other health issues. For example, skipping meals regularly or eating very small portions.

- **Purging:**

During purging, you may find someone getting rid of consumed calories, often after overeating. This can include self-induced vomiting, excessive exercise, or the misuse of laxatives or diuretics. For example, forcing oneself to vomit after eating to prevent weight gain.

Various types of eating disorders exist, and each one of them is characterized by distinct patterns of behavior and attitudes towards food. They include:

- **Anorexia Nervosa**

Individuals who have this disorder consistently maintain a weight below the average for their age and height. Children or adolescents with anorexia tend to experience an intense fear of gaining weight, which is often accompanied by a distorted body image. They end up perceiving themselves as overweight despite being very thin.

To stay underweight, they resort to harmful behaviors like starvation, sparse and infrequent eating, purging through vomiting or laxative use, and intense exercise. Many of these people are unaware of the unhealthy nature of these actions or the distorted way they perceive their bodies. Anorexia is an unhealthy coping mechanism for emotional problems, perfectionism, and a desire for control, with individuals often tying their self-worth to thinness. This disorder often causes other mental health issues like mood disorders or anxiety.

This disorder causes symptoms such as bluish discoloration of the fingers, hair thinning or falling out, soft body hair, exhaustion, sleeplessness, dizziness or fainting, and in teenage girls, the absence of menstruation.

- **Bulimia Nervosa**

People with this eating disorder experience episodes of bingeing and purging. During binge episodes, they consume a large amount of food, and afterward, they attempt to rid their bodies of the excess calories through purging behaviors. Purging methods they use include self-induced vomiting or engaging in extensive exercise, such as prolonged treadmill sessions.

Binge eating often occurs in private, which makes it challenging for others to notice the disorder. Despite engaging in these behaviors, individuals with bulimia may maintain an average or slightly overweight appearance, and this makes it less obvious that there's an issue.

This eating disorder typically begins in late adolescence or early adulthood and is more frequently diagnosed in women. Individuals with bulimia may also experience other mental health challenges like depression, anxiety, substance abuse, and self-harm tendencies.

Recognizable symptoms of bulimia may include discolored or stained teeth, calluses on the hands or knuckles from induced vomiting, swelling in the face, frequent weight fluctuations, and irregular menstrual cycles. Seeking professional help is crucial for those dealing with bulimia to address both the physical and mental aspects of the disorder.

- **Avoidant/Restrictive Food Intake Disorder**

When someone has restrictive or avoidant food intake problem, they find it difficult to eat specific foods because of its texture, color, taste, warmth, or aroma, among other sensory factors. The avoidance of particular foods is not motivated by a desire to lose weight, unlike anorexia nervosa.

Individuals with this disorder may have difficulties in maintaining a balanced diet. This may lead to consequences like weight loss, inadequate growth, and nutritional deficiencies. The impact of this disorder is not only physical but also psychosocial. For example, you will find someone struggling to eat with others, and this affects the way they socially interact around meals.

This eating disorder often begins in childhood, where a person may limit their food choices to an extremely narrow range and even reject familiar foods if they appear different. It can persist into adulthood and end up affecting various aspects of a person's life and health.

- **Binge Eating Disorder**

Binge eating disorder is when people regularly eat a lot of food, often in secret, without trying to get rid of the calories afterward. Even though they may feel embarrassed or guilty about it, they can't control the urge to eat excessively.

The fact that people with this illness might be overweight, obese, or of average weight makes it interesting. Besides struggling with binge eating, they may also have other mental health issues like depression. Handling emotions like anger, sadness, boredom, worry, and stress can be challenging for them.

While there might not be noticeable physical signs, binge eating disorder shows up through psychological symptoms like depression, anxiety, or feelings of shame and guilt about the amount of food eaten. Trying to lose weight through frequent dieting without success is another sign of this disorder.

- **Other Eating Disorders**

Not all children or adolescents neatly align with the mentioned diagnostic classifications, yet they may experience clinically significant eating-related issues. For instance, a teenager who doesn't engage in binge eating but consistently purges meals as a means to regulate weight or cope with emotions. Also, a child might exhibit night eating syndrome, characterized by the majority of caloric intake occurring from the later part of the day into the evening, with occasional instances of eating late at night.

Prevalence and Risk Factors

Eating disorders may happen to anyone at any time. Teenage years and early adulthood are common times when eating disorders first appear. However, they can happen at any age. The following factors may make an eating disorder more likely to occur:

- **Family history:**

A family history of eating disorders can increase the likelihood of a teenager developing similar issues. Genetic factors and learned behaviors within the family environment can lead to these disorders. Individuals with parents or siblings who have eating disorders face an increased risk of developing similar disorders themselves.

- **Age:**

Teens may be more susceptible to social pressures, body image issues, and the need for acceptance because of their developmental transitional stage. So, eating disorders may start as a result of the mentioned reasons.

- **Dieting and starvation:**

The pursuit of an idealized body image through extreme dieting or starvation can lead to unhealthy eating habits. Adolescents, influenced by societal standards, may engage in restrictive behaviors that lead to the development of eating disorders.

- **A history of weight bullying:**

Bullying or criticism about body weight can have long-term consequences for a teen's self-esteem and body image. This, in turn, may lead to disordered eating practices in an attempt to meet cultural expectations.

- **Life transitions:**

Major life transitions, such as moving to a new school, puberty, or changes in family dynamics, can create stress and emotional challenges. Teenagers may turn to disordered eating as a way to regain a sense of control during these transitions.

- **Extracurricular activities:**

The pressure to excel in certain extracurricular activities, especially those that emphasize physical appearance (e.g., dance, gymnastics, or modeling), may contribute to body dissatisfaction and an increased risk of developing eating disorders.

- **Stress:**

High levels of stress, whether academic, social, or personal, can contribute to the development of eating disorders. Teenagers may turn to unhealthy eating habits as a maladaptive coping mechanism to manage stress.

The Psychological Component

When someone has an eating disorder, there is usually an underlying psychological or mental health issue that contributes to their disorder. These underlying problems may encompass various aspects such as low self-esteem, where individuals might struggle with a negative perception of themselves. Depression and anxiety may also be factors since eating habits may be influenced by high levels of stress or persistent depressive feelings.

Also, obsessive-compulsive disorder (OCD) can contribute to the development or maintenance of eating disorders, involving repetitive thoughts and behaviors. Troubled relationships may serve as a source of emotional distress, potentially influencing one's relationship with food. Impulsive behavior can also contribute to erratic eating patterns and choices.

Recognizing the Telltale Signs of Disordered Eating

If your teen is dealing with an eating disorder, there are usually physical signs that you can notice. It's important to be able to see and understand these signs early on so you can get them the help and support they need.

- **Extreme weight loss or weight gain:**

You may notice a significant and rapid change in your child's body weight, either through a substantial loss or gain. Sudden and drastic weight fluctuations can be indicative of eating habits.

- **Fainting:**

If you find your child frequently experiencing episodes of fainting, it could be a red flag. Fainting can occur due to inadequate nutrition and insufficient energy intake, which is common in individuals with eating disorders.

- **Dizziness:**

Feeling lightheaded or dizzy, especially when standing up, may signal nutritional deficiencies that are resulting from irregular eating patterns or insufficient intake of essential nutrients.

- **Dry skin:**

Your child's skin may become noticeably dry and lacking in elasticity. Inadequate nutrition and dehydration can contribute to dry skin, as the body struggles to maintain its usual levels of hydration.

- **Brittle or dry hair:**

Pay attention to changes in the texture and quality of your child's hair. Brittle or excessively dry hair can be a consequence of nutritional deficiencies, particularly insufficient intake of vitamins and minerals.

- **Dental erosions:**

Eating disorders can lead to frequent vomiting, exposing teeth to stomach acids. Over time, this can result in dental erosions, characterized by the wearing away of tooth enamel.

- **Gastrointestinal distress:**

Your child might experience a range of gastrointestinal issues, such as bloating, constipation, or diarrhea. Disordered eating patterns can disrupt the normal functioning of the digestive system.

- **Chronic upper respiratory infections:**

Weakened immunity due to poor nutrition and overall physical stress can make your child more susceptible to recurrent upper respiratory infections, such as colds or flu.

- **Fine hair growing on the body:**

In response to nutritional deficiencies, your child's body may produce fine hair (known as lanugo) in an attempt to conserve heat. This is a noticeable yet subtle physical manifestation of an underlying issue.

Behavioral Patterns

When a teen is having eating disorders, you may start noticing some new behavioral patterns in their lives. These include:

- **Preoccupation with calories or nutrition:**

Your teen may find themselves constantly counting calories, meticulously tracking every morsel of food they consume, or obsessively researching nutritional information. Their thoughts often revolve around what they can or cannot eat, and they may feel anxious if they're unsure about the calorie content or nutritional value of certain foods.

- **Skipping meals:**

Your teen might intentionally skip meals as a way to control their weight or compensate for overeating. Skipping meals becomes a regular occurrence, and they may rationalize it by convincing themselves that they're not hungry or that they'll eat later, but in reality, they're avoiding food altogether.

- **Only eating certain foods/food groups:**

They may restrict their diet to a narrow range of foods or eliminate entire food groups, such as carbohydrates or fats. They may believe that certain foods are "good" or "bad," and they strictly adhere to these self-imposed dietary rules, often at the expense of balanced nutrition.

- **Displaying anxiety around eating:**

Your teen may feel anxious or distressed about mealtimes, experiencing heightened emotions or discomfort when faced with food. Eating in front of others may trigger feelings of anxiety or guilt, leading them to avoid social situations that involve food.

- **Patterns of binge eating or emotional eating:**

Sometimes people eat a lot of food really quickly, and they feel like they can't stop themselves. This is called *binge eating*. It might happen when they're feeling really upset, and they use food to try to feel better for a little while. But it's like a temporary fix because the bad feelings come back later.

- **Presence of laxative abuse:**

Your teen may resort to using laxatives as a means of purging or controlling their weight, even though it can have harmful effects on their digestive system and overall health. Laxative abuse is often a secretive behavior, and they may try to conceal their use of laxatives from others.

- **Frequent body-checking behaviors:**

They may constantly scrutinize their body in mirrors or reflective surfaces, seeking reassurance or validation about their appearance. They may also frequently weigh themselves or measure various body parts as a way to monitor changes in their weight or shape.

- **Wearing loose or baggy clothing:**

Your teen may prefer to wear loose-fitting clothing to conceal their body shape or size, feeling uncomfortable or self-conscious about their appearance in tighter garments. Baggy clothing can serve as a way to camouflage their body and avoid scrutiny from others.

- **Lying about food consumption:**

They may lie or withhold information about what they've eaten, either exaggerating the amount of food consumed to justify their behaviors or denying food intake altogether. Lying about food consumption is a common tactic used to conceal disordered eating habits from friends and family.

- **Exercising excessively:**

Your teen may engage in intense or prolonged exercise regimens with the primary goal of burning calories or compensating for food consumed. Exercise becomes an obsession, and they may prioritize it above all else, even at the expense of their physical health or social life.

Emotional Warning Signs

When observing your teen, it's important to pay close attention to emotional cues that could potentially indicate the presence of an eating disorder. Your teen may not always express their struggles verbally, but certain changes in behavior can serve as signals. Here are some key emotional cues to be aware of:

- **A change in eating habits:**

Keep an eye out for any noticeable alterations in your teen's eating patterns. This could involve a significant decrease or increase in food intake. For example, if your teen suddenly starts restricting their food intake, avoids meals, or exhibits an obsession with calorie counting, it might be indicative of an eating disorder.

- **Becoming very interested in food:**

On the other side, an unusual fixation or preoccupation with food can also be a cause for concern. If your teen becomes overly focused on meal planning, cooking elaborate dishes, or constantly discussing food-related topics, it may suggest a heightened and potentially unhealthy relationship with food.

- **Social withdrawal:**

Watch for signs of social withdrawal in your teen. If they start isolating themselves from friends and family, avoiding social events, or retreating to their room more frequently, it could be an emotional response linked to an eating disorder. Changes in social behavior may be an attempt to conceal their struggles or a reflection of internal distress.

- **Changes in mood, especially linked to eating:**

Pay attention to any noticeable shifts in your teen's mood, particularly surrounding mealtimes. Emotional distress related to eating may manifest as anxiety, irritability, or sadness. If your teen consistently displays negative emotions before, during, or after meals, it might be an emotional cue indicating an underlying struggle with an eating disorder.

Unraveling the Impact of Social Media on Eating Disorders

The Influence of Social Media

Feeling unhappy about your body can make some teenagers change the way they eat. This happens more with girls. Spending a lot of time on social media can make this feeling worse and increase the chances of developing eating disorders. How teenagers use photo-based social media like Instagram or Snapchat can affect their risk of having eating problems. Research shows that using social media more, especially on platforms like Facebook or Instagram, can make teenagers more likely to skip meals or exercise too much. Many teenagers, especially girls, spend a lot of time on Instagram, which seems to have the biggest impact. This can make them feel like they need to look a certain way, even if it's not realistic. Disturbingly, 52% of girls and 45% of boys resort to skipping meals and excessive exercise, with 75% of girls and 70% of boys having at least one social media account—Instagram being the most prevalent (Rapaport, 2019).

Social media often shows pictures of people who look perfect, which can make teenagers feel bad about themselves. They see these images and think they should look like that too, even though most of those pictures are edited to look perfect. Also, social media ads and posts sometimes promote unhealthy diets or products that promise quick weight loss. Influencers on social media often push these ideas, making teenagers feel like they need to change their bodies to fit in.

Social media algorithms often show thin or perfect-looking people more often, which can make teenagers think that's how they should look to be successful or liked. This can lead to teenagers having the wrong idea about what a healthy body looks like and doing things that are bad for them, like extreme diets or exercising too much. Communities on social media sometimes encourage these unhealthy habits, making it even harder for teenagers to feel good about themselves.

Comparison and Control

The carefully edited content that floods these platforms often showcases idealized body images, lifestyles, and beauty standards, creating unrealistic expectations. Constant exposure to such content cultivates a culture of comparison, where teens measure themselves against these unattainable ideals, which leads to a high sense of inadequacy.

Social media also perpetuates the idea that one's worth is intrinsically tied to physical appearance. This leads to a constant need for validation and acceptance. Users, particularly teens, may internalize the idea that conforming to societal beauty standards is essential for social approval.

In the pursuit of the perceived 'perfect' body, social media platforms also create the desire for control over one's body and food intake. Influencers and trends promoting specific diets, fitness routines, and beauty ideals contribute to the belief that strict control over these aspects is necessary for success and happiness. This desire for control can lead to the development of unhealthy eating habits, disordered eating, and in extreme cases, eating disorders.

Triggering Content

On social media, there's a lot more information about dieting, losing weight, and changing your body. This can be a big problem for people who already feel bad about how they look or have trouble with eating. You see, there's a lot of pictures, videos, and messages that make it seem like everyone should be super skinny and perfect. But the truth is that a lot of these ideas are not healthy at all.

For people who are already feeling down about themselves, seeing this content can make them feel even worse. It can make them start doing things like eating too little or exercising too much, which isn't good for them. Looking at all these pictures of people who seem perfect can make someone feel like they're not good enough, no matter what they do. It's like they're always chasing after a body that's impossible to have.

And it's not just the pictures and videos that are a problem — people also talk about this stuff in comments and groups online, making it seem like it's normal to feel bad about yourself or to do extreme things to change how you look.

This can make it even harder for someone to feel good about themselves or to get help if they need it. So, while social media can be fun, it's important to be careful about what you see and remember that nobody's perfect—and that's totally okay.

Feeding Hope: Strategies for Early Intervention and Empowering Recovery

Early Intervention

Detecting these conditions early can significantly improve treatment outcomes and reduce long-term health consequences. To initiate conversations and seek professional help for someone struggling with an eating disorder, follow these guidelines:

Talking to someone about their eating disorder:

- Choose a moment when both you and the person are calm and free from distractions. A private setting can create a safe space for open communication.

- Clearly express your observations and concerns about their well-being. Use "I" statements to avoid sounding accusatory, emphasizing your care and support.

- Understand that individuals with eating disorders may initially deny or resist acknowledging the issue. Approach the conversation with empathy and avoid placing blame.

- Encourage a dialogue about their feelings, motivations, and fears. Understanding their perspective can foster a collaborative approach to seeking help.

- Accept that change is a process that could require some time. Provide continuous assistance and motivate the individual to contemplate obtaining expert assistance from a therapist, counselor, or medical professional.

However, there are important considerations on what not to do.

- Avoid issuing ultimatums, as they may worsen the emotional turmoil.

- Refrain from commenting on the person's appearance or weight, as this can contribute to feelings of shame.

- Shaming and blaming should be avoided, as they hinder open communication.

- Lastly, resist the temptation to provide simplistic solutions, as eating disorders are complex mental health issues that require professional intervention.

Treatment Options

Treatment for eating disorders typically involves a multifaceted approach, suited to individual needs.

- Firstly, psychotherapy, such as cognitive-behavioral therapy (CBT), helps address unhealthy thoughts and behaviors surrounding food and body image.

- Nutritional counseling assists in establishing balanced eating habits and addressing nutritional deficiencies.

- Medical monitoring maintains stability in physical health and handles difficulties.

- Involving family members in the therapeutic process is essential for teenagers receiving family-based therapy.

- Doctors might give you certain medications, like pills for feeling sad or anxious, to help you deal with mental health issues.

- Lastly, support groups and peer networks provide ongoing encouragement and understanding.

A comprehensive treatment plan, often combining these modalities, promotes long-term recovery from eating disorders.

Interactive Activity

Encourage your teens to express gratitude to their bodies through a heartfelt thank-you letter. Prompt them to recall moments when their bodies supported them, urging them to delve beyond surface-level appreciation. By asking, "Can you remember a time when your body had your back?" you inspire introspection and gratitude. Initially, the notes may seem superficial, but with gentle encouragement, teens can unearth deep connections.

Encouraging this practice leads to a positive relationship between teens and their bodies, promoting self-love and appreciation. It empowers them to recognize their bodies' resilience, strength, and support in navigating life's challenges. Your guidance in this exercise cultivates a deeper understanding of self-care and gratitude, nurturing your teen's holistic health.

In conclusion, creating a supportive and non-judgmental environment is crucial for teens with eating disorders. Your empathy, validation, and encouragement are powerful tools for their recovery. Understand the complexity of these disorders, including their impact on eating habits and body image. Encourage gratitude towards their bodies to build self-esteem. Stay vigilant for signs of trouble and initiate sensitive conversations. Early intervention is key to success. Support teens through therapy, counseling, and medical care, providing essential resources for their journey to recovery. Your support can impact their well-being as they navigate the challenges of eating disorders.

In the upcoming chapter, you'll learn all about social anxiety disorder in teens and get useful tips to assist them in handling their symptoms, boosting their confidence in social situations, and dealing with them more comfortably.

Breaking Free: Conquering Social Anxiety in Adolescence

It's sad, actually, because my anxiety keeps me from enjoying things as much as I should in this age. —Amanda Seyfried

Invisible Shackles: Understanding Social Anxiety Disorder

Individuals with social anxiety suffer great anxiety or fear in social situations because they are afraid of being judged, receiving negative feedback, or being rejected. This anxiety can emerge in a variety of ways, including concerns about appearing worried or being seen adversely. People with social anxiety often avoid social interactions or performance situations, and when they cannot avoid them, they may experience significant distress. There are many signs you can use to tell that your child is struggling with social anxiety. Teens with social anxiety disorder may exhibit the following signs and symptoms:

- Extreme difficulty having normal conversations with other people

- Avoiding social settings where attention will be focused on them

- Finding it hard to talk to others

- Having anxiety, knowing they need to interact with other people, particularly if they don't know those people well

- Not being able to catch their breath

- Feelings of self-consciousness

- Feeling uncomfortable around others

- Having an intense fear of being embarrassed

- Blanking during social events

- Feeling embarrassed during interactions with other people

- Being very critical of themselves after social events and social interaction

- Worrying excessively for days, or even weeks, before social or public events

- Having an intense fear of being judged

- Low self-esteem

- Avoiding social situations and public places

- Shaking, sweating, blushing, or having an accelerated heartbeat in social settings

- Finding it difficult to make friends

- Finding it challenging to maintain relationships

- Having stomachaches or nausea when being around others

- Feeling confused in social settings

- Having diarrhea or muscle tension around others

Impact on Adolescents

When teens are dealing with social anxiety disorder, there are a bunch of tough things they might face. First off, there's the loneliness. It can feel like they're always on the outside looking in, even when they're surrounded by people. Their self-esteem might take a hit too. They might constantly doubt themselves and feel like they're not good enough.

Then, there are academic issues. It can be really hard to concentrate and participate in class when these teens are anxious about what people think of them. Their grades might suffer as a result.

Plus, when they're always stressed, they might neglect their health. They might not eat right, exercise enough, or get enough sleep, which can make everything feel even harder.

And it doesn't stop there. Social anxiety disorder can lead to depression. When they're constantly worried about social situations, it can wear them down emotionally, making them feel sad and hopeless. They might even become a target for bullying because bullies can sense vulnerability. This can make everything feel even more overwhelming.

All of this can create tension at home too. They might argue more with their family because they don't understand what they're going through, or they might withdraw from them altogether. So, yeah, social anxiety disorder isn't just about feeling nervous in social situations—it can affect every aspect of their life.

Facing the Fear: Navigating Triggers of Social Anxiety

As your teen or child navigates through adolescence, there are various situations and factors that can intensify their social anxiety. These include:

- **Parenting styles**: How you, as a parent, approach and interact with your teen can significantly impact their social anxiety levels. Overly strict or critical parenting styles may contribute to high levels of anxiety in social situations.

- **Genetics**: Your teen's genetic makeup can play a role in their predisposition to social anxiety. If there's a family history of anxiety disorders, your teen may be more susceptible to experiencing social anxiety themselves.

- **Peer pressure**: The pressure to fit in and conform to social norms among their peers can trigger or exacerbate social anxiety in your teen. Feeling the need to meet certain expectations or fearing rejection from peers can be overwhelming.

- **Bullying**: Experiencing bullying, whether in person or online, can deeply affect your teen's confidence and sense of safety in social settings, leading to increased anxiety.

- **Sleep deprivation**: Lack of sufficient sleep can exacerbate feelings of stress and anxiety in your teen, making it more challenging for them to cope with social situations effectively.

- **Hormonal changes**: When you're a teenager, your hormones can go up and down a lot, which can make your mood change quickly and make you feel more sensitive to things. This can sometimes make social situations feel harder to handle, and you might feel more anxious about being around other people.

- **Brain development**: The ongoing development of the teenage brain can influence how your teen processes social situations and emotions, impacting their susceptibility to social anxiety.

- **Using drugs and alcohol**: Substance use can exacerbate social anxiety symptoms in teens, as they may rely on substances to cope with social situations or to alleviate their anxiety temporarily.

- **Depression**: Teens with depression are more likely to experience social anxiety, as feelings of low self-worth and hopelessness can intensify their fears of social interaction and judgment.

- **Technology devices**: Excessive use of technology, particularly social media, can contribute to feelings of isolation, comparison, and inadequacy in your teen, fueling social anxiety.

Cognitive Distortions

Cognitive distortions are like tricks our minds play on us, making us see things in a negative or inaccurate way. They're common among people of all ages, but teenagers can be particularly affected. It's normal for teens to feel down or upset sometimes, but when these negative thoughts keep popping up, they can lead to even more negative feelings and behaviors.

Teens are still learning how to handle their emotions and thoughts, so it's important to catch these distorted thoughts early. If left unchecked, they can contribute to problems like anxiety or depression. Teenagers often feel emotions really strongly, which can make it tough for them to deal with tricky situations.

Recognizing these distorted thoughts and helping teens learn how to challenge them is super important. It's like giving them tools to handle tough times and feel better about themselves. By understanding and managing these thoughts, teens can learn to navigate life's ups and downs in a healthier way.

The different types include:

- **Mind reading**:

This is when teenagers assume they know what someone else is thinking without any evidence to support their assumption. They often interpret these assumed thoughts negatively, believing that others are judging or criticizing them in some way. For example, if a friend doesn't respond to a text message right away, a teen might assume they're being ignored or disliked.

- **Future-telling**:

Future-telling involves predicting negative outcomes for future events without considering other, more positive possibilities. Teenagers with this distortion often expect the worst to happen, which can lead to anxiety and avoidance behaviors. For instance, a teen might predict that they'll fail a test before even studying for it, leading them to give up before even trying.

- **Catastrophizing**:

This distortion involves exaggerating the importance or severity of problems or negative events. Teenagers may blow minor setbacks out of proportion, viewing them as catastrophic failures. For example, failing a single test might lead a teen to believe they'll never succeed in school or life.

- **Labeling**:

Labeling occurs when teenagers assign overly simplistic and negative labels to themselves or others, reducing their identities or character to these labels. Instead of seeing the complexity and nuance of individuals, teens might categorize themselves or others as "stupid," "worthless," or "bad." This can lead to rigid thinking and affect how they interact with themselves and others.

- **Overgeneralizing**:

Overgeneralizing involves taking one negative event or aspect of a situation and applying it to all aspects of life. For example, if a teenager fails a test, they might conclude that they're a failure in general and will never succeed at anything. This can lead to a sense of hopelessness and low self-esteem.

- **All-or-nothing thinking**:

Sometimes, people have this way of thinking where they only see things as either all good or all bad, with no in-between. Teenagers who think like this don't really see any middle ground in situations. For instance, if they're not the absolute best at something, they might think they're total failures. It's like they can't see shades of gray; everything's either black or white to them.

- **Blaming**:

Blaming involves attributing one's own negative feelings or circumstances to external factors, usually other people. Instead of taking responsibility for their own actions and emotions, teenagers with this distortion may blame others for their problems, which can lead to conflict and strained relationships.

- **Personalization**:

Personalization happens when teens think that things that happen around them are all about them, even if they're not. For instance, if a friend cancels hanging out, a teen might feel like it's because of something they did, even if it's not their fault at all. This kind of thinking can make them feel bad about themselves for no reason, like they're to blame for everything.

Negative thought patterns and cognitive distortions play a significant role in the development and maintenance of social anxiety. These patterns involve habitual ways of thinking that are biased and unrealistic, leading individuals to perceive social situations in a distorted and often exaggerated manner. There are many ways you can recognize cognitive distortions in teens, and they include:

- **Negative self-talk**: Constantly being hard on yourself and always pointing out what you think are your faults or mistakes is what we call *negative self-talk*. It's like having a little voice inside your head that keeps telling you that you're not good enough or that you're doing everything wrong. When you keep hearing these negative thoughts, it can make you feel like you're not as good as others and can make you really anxious about being around people.

- **Excessive perfectionism**: When teens set unrealistically high standards for themselves and become overly focused on avoiding mistakes, it can lead to anxiety about not meeting these standards in social situations. Fear of not being perfect can result in avoidance of social interactions altogether.

- **Emotional overreactions**: Teens may experience intense emotional responses to social situations, such as extreme fear of embarrassment or rejection. These overreactions can stem from distorted beliefs about the importance of social acceptance and the potential consequences of social mishaps.

- **Social withdrawal**: Avoiding social interactions can become a coping mechanism for teens experiencing social anxiety. They may isolate themselves to avoid potential judgment or embarrassment, which only serves to reinforce their fears and negative beliefs about social interactions.

- **Constant comparison to others**: Teens with social anxiety often engage in constant comparison with their peers, leading to feelings of inadequacy and inferiority. This comparison can exacerbate negative self-talk and contribute to a sense of not measuring up socially.

- **Difficulty accepting compliments**: Teens with social anxiety may struggle to accept compliments because they have difficulty believing positive feedback about themselves. They may dismiss compliments or feel uncomfortable receiving praise, reinforcing negative self-perceptions.

- **Self-blame**: When social interactions don't go as planned, teens with social anxiety may blame themselves excessively. This self-blame reinforces negative beliefs about their social abilities and can increase anxiety about future interactions.

- **Avoidance of challenges**: Teens may avoid challenging social situations or new experiences out of fear of failure or embarrassment. This avoidance prevents them from developing essential social skills and reinforces their belief that they are incapable or inadequate in social settings.

Avoidance Behaviors

Avoidance behaviors are actions or inactions that teenagers engage in to alleviate their anxiety about being in social situations. However, these behaviors are problematic because, in the long term, they only serve to reinforce and heighten their fear of social interactions. Avoidance behaviors can manifest in three main forms: avoidance, escape, or partial avoidance.

1. **Avoidance**: This involves completely avoiding the feared social situation. For instance, a teenager who is afraid of public speaking might drop a class where they have to give a speech, change jobs to avoid presentations, or even fail to attend events like weddings or awards ceremonies where they are expected to speak in front of others.

2. **Escape**: When total avoidance is not possible, teens may resort to escape behaviors as a way of coping with their anxiety. Escape entails leaving or exiting from a social or performance situation that is causing distress. For example, a teen might leave a gathering early, walk out during a speech, or retreat to the restroom during a dinner party to alleviate their discomfort.

3. **Partial Avoidance**: When neither avoidance nor escape is feasible, teens may resort to partial avoidance, also known as safety behaviors, to

manage their anxiety during social or performance situations. Safety behaviors aim to control or limit their experience of the situation. Examples of partial avoidance include avoiding eye contact, reducing verbal communication, or speaking softly to minimize attention.

These avoidance behaviors may provide temporary relief from anxiety, but they ultimately reinforce the belief that social situations are threatening and uncontrollable. Over time, reliance on avoidance behaviors can lead to further impairment in social functioning and exacerbate social anxiety symptoms. In addressing social anxiety in teens, it's crucial to recognize these avoidance patterns and work towards gradually exposing them to feared social situations while teaching coping strategies to manage anxiety effectively without resorting to avoidance. Therapy, particularly cognitive-behavioral approaches, can help teens challenge these avoidance behaviors and develop more adaptive ways of coping with social anxiety.

Empowering Strategies for Overcoming Social Anxiety

Coping Skills

Having ways to deal with feeling anxious around others is really important for teenagers. Here are some tips that can help teens handle tough social situations better:

First off, it's helpful to challenge those negative thoughts that make you worried about social stuff. Try figuring out what those thoughts are and then questioning if they're really true. This can help you see that some of your fears might not be as big as they seem, which can make you feel more confident.

Another good idea is to focus more on other people instead of just thinking about yourself. Pay attention to what others are saying and try to join in conversations. Remember, most people are more worried about themselves than they are of judging you.

Learning to control your breathing can also help calm you down when you're feeling anxious. Trying things like deep breathing exercises can make you feel more relaxed in stressful situations. Just remember, it might take some practice to get the hang of it.

Getting out there and being social, even if it's a bit scary at first, can really help too. Start by doing small social things and work your way up to bigger ones. Taking these small steps outside your comfort zone can help you feel more confident.

Lastly, taking care of yourself is super important. Make sure to eat well, exercise, and get enough sleep. And try out things like mindfulness or relaxation exercises to help keep stress in check. Taking care of yourself overall can make a big difference in how you handle social anxiety.

How to Support Teens With Anxiety

Helping teens deal with anxiety, especially when it comes to social situations, needs a comprehensive plan. It's not just about talking through feelings; it's also about giving practical support. Here are some simple tips for how you can help teens with social anxiety:

- **Discuss the Evolutionary Origins of Anxiety**: Start by explaining to teens that anxiety is a natural and adaptive response that has evolutionary origins. Help them understand that anxiety served a protective function in our ancestors by alerting them to potential threats in their environment. This normalization can reduce stigma and help teens recognize that their anxiety is not a sign of weakness.

- **Teach Calming Techniques**: Give teenagers simple ways to deal with their anxiety right away. This might mean teaching them stuff like taking deep breaths, relaxing their muscles one by one, or doing mindfulness exercises. These things can help calm them down when they're feeling stressed out. Encourage them to practice these exercises often so they can use them whenever they start feeling anxious. It's like having a toolbox of techniques to help them feel better when things get tough.

- **Gather More Information**: Talk openly with your teenager about what's bothering them. Ask them about the things that make them anxious or scared and listen carefully without judging. Try to understand why they feel this way and what situations make it worse. This helps both of you figure out where they need help and what can be done to make things better.

- **Adjust Expectations**: It's important to help teens understand that it's okay not to be perfect and to have realistic expectations for themselves and their friendships. Instead of aiming for perfection, they should focus on making progress, even if it's small steps. Feeling anxious at times is normal, and they shouldn't be too hard on themselves about it. By setting goals they can actually reach and being proud of even the little successes, teens can feel more confident and better able to handle their anxiety.

- **Problem Solving**: Work together with your teen to figure out solutions and ways to handle tough social situations. Sit down and talk about ideas on how to deal with these problems, and then let your teen try out different ways to see what works best. This helps them feel like they're in control and learning how to handle their anxiety better. Plus, it teaches them how to solve problems, which will come in handy later on.

- **Conquering Negative Thoughts**: You need to show teens how to deal with negative thoughts that make them anxious. Help them spot these thoughts, like thinking the worst will happen or assuming what others think, and then replace them with more reasonable ones. This way, they can train their brains to think in a more positive and sensible way, which can make them feel better overall. This process is called *cognitive restructuring*, and it helps teens build a healthier mindset.

- **Model Social Behavior**: As a parent or caregiver, model healthy social behavior and coping strategies for managing stress and anxiety. Demonstrate effective communication skills, self-regulation techniques, and resilience in navigating social situations. Your own behavior can serve as a powerful example and provide teens with valuable guidance and support.

By using these ideas in how you help teens, you can make it easier for them to handle feeling nervous in social situations and get better at being around others. Just remember to be understanding, caring, and always there for them when they need you. And if things seem really tough, don't hesitate to get help from a pro to make sure they get all the support they need to feel better.

Helping teens deal with anxiety requires being understanding, patient, and caring. It's important to make them feel safe and comfortable so they can talk about how they feel and ask for help when they need it. When you're supporting a teen with anxiety, there are certain things you shouldn't do. These include:

1. **Criticizing**: Criticizing a teen with anxiety can worsen their symptoms and undermine their self-esteem. Teens with anxiety often already have a heightened sense of self-criticism and fear of failure. Criticism can reinforce their negative beliefs about themselves and their abilities, exacerbating their anxiety. Instead, it's essential to offer constructive feedback and praise their efforts, focusing on their strengths rather than their shortcomings.

2. **Labeling as Shy**: Labeling a teen as "shy" can be detrimental because it oversimplifies their experience and overlooks the complexity of anxiety. While shyness may be a component of social anxiety, labeling a teen in this way can minimize the seriousness of their condition and discourage them from seeking help. It's important to recognize that anxiety is a legitimate mental health issue that requires understanding and support, regardless of whether the teen exhibits shy behavior.

3. **Blaming**: Blaming a teen for their anxiety only adds to their feelings of guilt and inadequacy. Anxiety is not a choice, and teens with anxiety are not to blame for their condition. Blaming them can make them feel misunderstood and invalidated, further isolating them from support. Instead of assigning blame, it's

crucial to offer empathy, reassurance, and practical assistance in managing their anxiety.

4. **Accommodating Avoidance**: Allowing teens to avoid anxiety-provoking situations may provide temporary relief, but it reinforces avoidance behaviors in the long run. Accommodating avoidance can prevent teens from developing effective coping strategies and ultimately worsen their anxiety. Instead, it's important to encourage teens to face their fears gradually and provide support and encouragement as they navigate challenging situations. By gradually exposing them to feared situations in a supportive environment, teens can learn to manage their anxiety and build resilience over time.

All in all, supporting teens with anxiety requires avoiding criticism, refraining from labeling, abstaining from blame, and discouraging accommodation of avoidance behaviors. Instead, it's essential to offer understanding, empathy, and practical support to help teens manage their anxiety and build resilience for the future.

Interactive Element

Cognitive Restructuring

Cognitive restructuring is a therapeutic technique that helps teens challenge and change their negative thought patterns and beliefs. By identifying and replacing unhelpful thoughts with more balanced and realistic ones, teens can alleviate distress and improve their mental well-being. This process involves recognizing cognitive distortions, questioning their validity, and generating alternative perspectives.

Worksheet Prompts for Teens:

1. Identify a recent social situation that made you anxious. What negative thoughts did you have about yourself in that moment?

2. Reflect on a time when you avoided a social activity due to fear. What were you telling yourself about the situation?

3. Describe a thought that often pops into your mind when meeting new people. Is it helpful or unhelpful?

4. Think about a past social event where you felt uncomfortable. What were you assuming about others' perceptions of you?

5. Recall a compliment you received recently. Did you have any doubts or negative thoughts about accepting it?

6. Consider a situation where you compared yourself to someone else. What negative beliefs did you hold about yourself?

7. Imagine a future social event you're worried about. What catastrophizing thoughts are you having?

8. Reflect on a time when you blamed yourself for a social mishap. What could be an alternative explanation?

9. Think about a challenge you avoided due to fear of failure. What were you predicting about the outcome?

10. Describe a situation where you personalized someone's behavior towards you. How might you reinterpret their actions in a less negative light?

In conclusion, creating supportive and inclusive environments where teenagers with social anxiety feel accepted and valued is paramount for their well-being. Such environments should be free from judgment or stigma, allowing teens to express themselves authentically without fear of ridicule or rejection. Recognizing the challenges faced by teens with social anxiety, including loneliness, diminished self-esteem, academic struggles, and potential depression, underscores the importance of providing compassionate support and understanding. Empowering teens with coping skills, challenging negative thought patterns, and fostering resilience can help them navigate social situations with greater confidence and ease. By addressing social anxiety in a holistic manner and promoting a culture of acceptance and support, we can create a more inclusive society where all teenagers feel empowered to thrive.

In the next chapter, you'll learn all about cyberbullying and how it affects teens' mental health. We'll dive deep into how common cyberbullying is and how it can really mess with how teens feel.

Digital Dangers: Battling Cyberbullying in the Online World

Cyber bullies can hide behind a mask of anonymity online, and do not need direct physical access to their victims to do unimaginable harm. –Anna Maria Chavez

The Dark Side of Screens: Unveiling the Impact of Cyberbullying

Cyberbullying is when someone harasses, threatens, or hurts other people using internet channels. It can take many different forms, such as posting cruel remarks, publishing embarrassing images or videos without consent, starting rumors, and pretending to be someone else online. Research shows that 59% of American teenagers have been the victim of internet bullying, highlighting the problem's frequency and effects on children (Anderson, 2018). Because of its extensive reach, anonymity, and round-the-clock accessibility, this type of bullying presents serious difficulties that exacerbate the suffering done to victims and underscore the pressing need for efficient preventative and intervention strategies.

There are very many types of cyberbullying. Each type of cyberbullying has its own methods and consequences, but they all share the common goal of causing harm, intimidation, or distress to the victim. These types include:

- **Exclusion**:

Exclusion involves intentionally leaving someone out of online activities, groups, or conversations. This can manifest in various forms, such as excluding someone from social media groups, online games, or group chats. Exclusion can be particularly harmful as it makes the victim feel isolated, rejected, and left out from their peer group, exacerbating feelings of loneliness and low self-esteem.

- **Harassment**:

Harassment refers to repeatedly sending offensive, threatening, or hurtful messages to an individual online. This can include sending abusive emails, text messages, or social media comments, as well as making derogatory posts or sharing humiliating content about the victim. Harassment can cause significant emotional distress, fear, and anxiety for the victim, leading to psychological harm and impaired well-being.

- **Cyberstalking**:

Cyberstalking involves the persistent monitoring, tracking, or surveillance of an individual's online activities without their consent. This can include tracking someone's location, accessing their personal information, or constantly monitoring their social media accounts. Cyberstalkers may also send threatening or intimidating messages, making the victim feel unsafe and vulnerable to harm.

- **Outing:**

Outing occurs when someone publicly shares private or sensitive information about an individual without their consent. This can include revealing someone's secrets, medical history, or other confidential information online. Outing can have devastating consequences for the victim, leading to embarrassment, humiliation, and social ostracism.

- **Doxxing:**

Doxxing involves publicly disclosing someone's personal information, such as their home address, phone number, or financial details, with the intent to harass, intimidate, or harm them. This information may be obtained through hacking, social engineering, or other means. Doxxing can pose serious safety and security risks for the victim, including identity theft, stalking, or physical harm.

- **Fraping:**

Fraping, short for "Facebook raping," refers to unauthorized access to someone's social media account, typically to post embarrassing or inappropriate content without their knowledge. This can include posting offensive status updates, sending inappropriate messages to friends, or altering profile information. Fraping undermines the victim's control over their online identity and can lead to embarrassment and reputational damage.

- **Trolling**:

Trolling involves deliberately provoking or antagonizing others online to elicit a strong emotional reaction. Trolls may engage in inflammatory or offensive behavior, such as posting inflammatory comments, spreading false information, or engaging in personal attacks. Trolling disrupts online communities, creates conflict, and can cause emotional distress for the victims.

- **Dissing**:

Dissing refers to publicly disrespecting or insulting someone online, often through derogatory comments, memes, or images. This can occur on social media platforms, online forums, or in chat rooms. Dissing undermines the victim's self-esteem and can lead to feelings of shame, embarrassment, and social isolation.

- **Flaming**:

Flaming involves engaging in hostile, aggressive, or abusive communication online, typically in the form of heated arguments or verbal attacks. This can occur in online discussions, forums, or comment sections, where individuals insult, belittle, or ridicule others. Flaming escalates conflicts, creates a hostile online environment, and can cause emotional harm to the targets.

- **Denigration**:

Denigration involves spreading false or malicious rumors or gossip about someone online with the intent to damage their reputation or social standing. This can include posting defamatory statements, spreading rumors, or sharing embarrassing photos or videos. Denigration can tarnish the victim's reputation, lead to social ostracism, and cause significant emotional distress.

- **Impersonation**:

Impersonation is the act of someone creating a false online persona or account in order to pass for someone else, frequently with the intention of tricking or controlling other people. This could involve impersonating someone online by exploiting their name, images, or private information. Identity theft, harm to one's reputation, and legal repercussions for the imposter are all possible outcomes of impersonation.

Here are some of the examples of cyberbullying:

- **Sending mean texts or emails**: This involves sending messages containing insults, threats, or derogatory remarks directly to the target's phone or email account. The anonymity and immediacy of texting and emailing make it easy for cyberbullies to harass their victims without facing immediate consequences.

- **Posting hurtful messages on social media**: Cyberbullies use social media platforms like Facebook, Twitter, Instagram, and Snapchat to publicly humiliate or shame their targets by posting hurtful comments, photos, or videos. These posts can reach a wide audience quickly, amplifying the emotional harm experienced by the victim.

- **Spreading rumors online**: Cyberbullies spread false or damaging information about their targets through social media, forums, or messaging apps. Rumors can damage a person's reputation, relationships, and self-esteem, causing significant emotional distress and social consequences for the victim.

- **Circulating false or embarrassing information about someone else**: This involves sharing personal or embarrassing details about someone without their consent, either publicly or privately. Cyberbullies may use this information to ridicule, embarrass, or blackmail their targets, leading to feelings of shame, humiliation, and vulnerability.

- **Posting or sharing private images**: Cyberbullies may post incriminating or personal images or videos of their victims without permission; this is sometimes referred to as "revenge porn." This invasion of privacy may have detrimental effects on the victim's personal and professional life, including psychological distress, social disgrace, and maybe legal action.

- **Impersonating someone online to hurt their reputation**: Cyberbullies impersonate their targets by creating fake social media profiles or email accounts in order to spread false information, harass them online, or destroy their reputation. This type of identity theft can cause confusion, harm relationships, and reduce the victim's credibility and reliability.

- **Excluding someone from an online group**: Cyberbullies may intentionally exclude or isolate individuals from online communities, group chats, or gaming sessions as a form of social rejection or ostracism. This exclusionary behavior can exacerbate feelings of loneliness, alienation, and social isolation in the victim.

- **Creating hate groups or websites against a particular person**: Cyberbullies may create online forums, blogs, or websites dedicated to spreading hate speech, derogatory comments, or threats against a specific individual or group. These hate groups can escalate cyberbullying behaviors, incite violence, and foster a toxic online environment that promotes intolerance and discrimination.

Overall, cyberbullying can have serious and long-lasting consequences for victims, including emotional trauma, social isolation, academic decline, and even suicidal ideation.

Effects on Mental Health

The effects of cyberbullying towards teens can either be Emotional, mental, behavioral, or physical. These effects shown below:

Emotional Effects of Cyberbullying:

- **Humiliation**: Being subjected to cyberbullying can lead to feelings of humiliation, as hurtful or embarrassing messages or posts are shared publicly online. This humiliation can be particularly devastating for teens who feel exposed and powerless to control the situation.

- **Isolation**: Cyberbullying often leads to social isolation as victims may withdraw from social interactions out of fear or embarrassment. They may also feel ostracized by their peers, which leads to feelings of loneliness and alienation.

- **Anger**: Teens who experience cyberbullying may feel a sense of anger towards their bullies, as well as towards themselves for being unable to prevent or stop the harassment. This anger can be overwhelming and may manifest in both online and offline interactions.

- **Powerlessness**: Cyberbullying can leave victims feeling powerless and vulnerable. They may struggle to regain control over their online reputation or stop the harassment, leading to a sense of helplessness and despair.

Mental Effects of Cyberbullying:

- **Depression and anxiety**: Cyberbullying is strongly associated with an increased risk of depression and anxiety among teenagers. Persistent harassment and negative messages can erode self-esteem and exacerbate feelings of sadness, hopelessness, and worthlessness.

- **Low self-esteem**: Constant exposure to cyberbullying can undermine a teenager's sense of self-worth and confidence. Negative comments and attacks on their appearance, abilities, or character can contribute to feelings of inadequacy and inferiority.

- **Academic issues**: Cyberbullying can have detrimental effects on a teen's academic performance and motivation. Victims may struggle to concentrate in school, experience declines in grades, or even avoid attending classes altogether due to fear of encountering their bullies.

- **Suicidal thoughts and self-harm**: Perhaps the most concerning aspect of cyberbullying is its association with suicidal thoughts and self-harming acts among teenagers. The unrelenting nature of online harassment can drive vulnerable people to the point of self-harm or suicide in order to escape the agony and shame.

Behavioral Effects of Cyberbullying

- **Using drugs or alcohol**: Victims of cyberbullying may turn to substance abuse to cope with the emotional discomfort created by the harassment. They may seek consolation in drugs or alcohol to alleviate their anguish or escape the continual worry and anxiety that comes with cyberbullying. Substance misuse can worsen their vulnerability and impair their judgment, resulting in risky behavior and negative effects.

- **Skipping school**: The relentless harassment and intimidation experienced through cyberbullying can make victims feel unsafe and unwelcome at school. As a result, they may develop a strong aversion to attending classes or participating in school-related activities. Chronic absenteeism due to cyberbullying can have significant academic consequences, including falling behind in coursework, lower grades, and ultimately, academic failure.

- **Carrying a weapon**: In extreme cases, victims of cyberbullying may resort to carrying weapons as a means of self-defense or retaliation against their aggressors. The constant threat of physical harm, coupled with feelings of powerlessness and vulnerability, may compel some individuals to arm themselves for protection. However, carrying weapons only escalates the risk of violence and poses a danger to both the victim and others, perpetuating a cycle of fear and aggression.

Physical Effects of Cyberbullying

- **Gastrointestinal issues**: Cyberbullying-induced stress and worry can cause physical symptoms such as stomachaches, nausea, and digestive disorders. Chronic stress impairs the digestive system's natural function, causing increased stomach acid, inflammation, and muscle tension. Persistent gastrointestinal disorders can have a substantial impact on the victim's quality of life and may necessitate medical intervention to resolve.

- **Disordered eating**: Cyberbullying victims may develop disordered eating behaviors as a response to the emotional turmoil inflicted by online harassment. Stress, anxiety, and low self-esteem can disrupt normal eating patterns and lead to unhealthy dietary habits such as binge eating, purging, or restrictive eating. These behaviors are maladaptive coping mechanisms to regain a sense of control or numb emotional pain but can have serious implications for the victim's physical and mental health.

- **Sleep disturbances**: Cyberbullying can disrupt sleep patterns and cause psychological distress, which can lead to insomnia, nightmares, and frequent awakenings. Chronic sleep deprivation can result from persistent feelings of anxiety, worry, or sadness that interfere with your ability to fall and stay asleep. Issues with sleep make it harder for the victim to deal with the effects of cyberbullying since they impair cognitive function and increase the victim's emotional vulnerability.

The prevalence of cyberbullying among teenagers poses a significant risk to mental health and overall well-being, a concern that is underscored by various statistics. Studies reveal that teenagers who fall victim to cyberbullying are four times more likely to engage in self-harming behaviors or consider suicide compared to those who have not experienced such harassment.

Also, a substantial 93% of cyberbullying victims report adverse mental health effects, primarily characterized by sadness and hopelessness. The repercussions extend beyond emotional distress, with approximately two-thirds of students acknowledging that cyberbullying significantly impairs their ability to learn and feel safe within their school environment (Cyberbullying: The Mental Health Impact and How to Help Your Teen, 2023).

Notably, the detrimental impact of cyberbullying is not limited to psychological consequences, as a third of victims also exhibit symptoms of stress, indicating physiological strain. Gender differences are apparent as well, with 66% of female victims expressing powerlessness that comes from cyberbullying incidents (Cyberbullying: The Mental Health Impact and How to Help Your Teen, 2023).

It's concerning to note that both victims and offenders of cyberbullying are more likely to suffer from poor self-esteem, which feeds a destructive cycle among teenage social networks. These results highlight how urgently comprehensive interventions and support systems are needed to successfully combat cyberbullying and lessen its detrimental impact on adolescent mental health and academic performance.

Long-Term Consequences

When cyberbullying isn't stopped, it can affect people for a long time. But if victims can get help fast and have people who support them, it can make things better. If nothing is done to help, kids might suffer for a long time, which can affect how they feel overall. Cyberbullying also makes it more likely that victims will think about hurting themselves or even try to do so, which is really dangerous. It can also lead to other problems like feeling really scared or stressed all the time, which can make it hard to do normal things. Cyberbullying can even make people feel sick because it causes so much stress and worry. So, it's important to stop cyberbullying and help those who are going through it to feel better and stay safe.

Sometimes, when people are bullied online, it can have serious effects on them. They might start doing harmful things to themselves like hurting themselves or using drugs. Cyberbullying can also make it hard for them to trust others or make friends, which can make them feel really lonely. It's important to act quickly when someone is being cyberbullied to stop it from getting worse. Giving them support, finding them help, and making sure they get the mental health support they need can help them get through it and feel better.

Bytes of Betrayal: Understanding Technology's Role in Cyberbullying

Social Media Dynamic

Social media is often used for bullying, which can be really hurtful, maybe even worse than when it happens in person. Unlike when people bully face-to-face, online bullying can happen without anyone knowing who's doing it. This means bullies can say mean things without getting caught. They can reach lots of people all at once, making it even harder for the person being bullied. Because they can hide their identity, bullies feel more confident and can pick on others without worrying about getting into trouble.

Cyberbullying on social media is a big problem with many different sides to it. Bullies can use lots of ways to hurt others, like spreading rumors, sharing embarrassing pictures, or sending mean messages. This kind of bullying can really hurt someone's feelings and make them feel awful. And because social media is so fast and reaches lots of people, it's hard for the person being bullied to get away from it.

Even though cyberbullying happens a lot, social media sites don't always do enough to stop it. They often don't have good ways for people to report bullying, so bullies don't face consequences for what they do. Plus, there's so much stuff on social media that it's tough for the sites to keep an eye on everything and stop the mean stuff from happening.

A study by the Pew Research Center found that many teenagers see cyberbullying happening but feel like nobody does much about it. Most of them think social media sites aren't doing a good job stopping it. This makes people feel helpless and upset, and the bullying just keeps happening.

In the end, social media makes cyberbullying worse because it's easy to use, people can stay anonymous, and it's hard to stop. Fixing this problem needs both social media companies and everyone else to work together to make online spaces safer and make bullies take responsibility for what they do.

Anonymous Platforms

As already mentioned, being anonymous online can make some people feel brave enough to say mean things or do bad stuff to others. They think they won't get caught because nobody knows who they are. This false sense of courage lets them act in ways they wouldn't if they were talking face-to-face with someone. They might use fake names or hide behind fake accounts, making it hard for anyone to figure out who's doing the bullying.

Cyberbullying is tough to deal with because it's hard to know who's doing it. Unlike bullying in real life where you might know who's bothering you, online bullies can hide their identity easily. This makes it tricky for victims and even the authorities to figure out who's behind the mean behavior. So, stopping cyberbullies is a tough job because finding out who they are and collecting evidence against them takes a lot of time and effort.

Online Safety Measures

Report Cyberbullying

Cyberbullying can have serious consequences, but there are steps you can take to address it effectively:

- **Immediate actions:**

If someone is bullying you online, it's best not to respond to them. Talking back to cyberbullies can make things worse and might make them harass you even more. Ignoring them can help stop the situation from getting worse and prevent more conflict.

Make sure to keep proof of the cyberbullying. Keep track of when it happens, what was said, and any other details. This evidence can be really important if you need to report the bullying to someone who can help. Saving screenshots or messages can show exactly what's been going on and prove that you're being bullied.

You can also block the bully. Most social media and messaging apps have a block feature. Blocking them means they can't contact you anymore, which can help you feel safer online. It's a way to take control and make sure you don't have to deal with their hurtful messages anymore.

- **Report to online service providers:**

If you're facing cyberbullying, it's important to report it to the websites or social media networks where it's happening. They usually have ways for you to report this kind of behavior, and it helps them enforce their rules and keep everyone safe online.

Show proof of what's happening. When you report cyberbullying, it's helpful to have evidence to back up your claim. This could be screenshots of mean messages, emails, or texts. Giving these to the website or platform makes it easier for them to see what's going on and do something about it quickly. Showing proof makes your report stronger and increases the chances of the bully facing consequences for their actions.

- **Report to law enforcement:**

If cyberbullying gets really serious and involves threats or harassment, it's important to think about getting the police involved. Law enforcement agencies have the power to look into cyberbullying cases and take legal action against the people causing trouble. So, if you're feeling scared or in danger because of cyberbullying, don't hesitate to reach out to the police.

When you talk to the police, it's helpful to have evidence of what's been happening. This could be screenshots of mean messages or any other proof you've gathered. The police need this evidence to start their investigation and figure out what to do next. So, if you decide to involve law enforcement, make sure you give them all the information you have. Working together with the police can help put a stop to the cyberbullying and make things safer for you.

- **Report to schools:**

Tell the school about it. If cyberbullying involves students, it's important to let the school know so they can deal with it properly. Schools have rules and ways to help students who are being cyberbullied. By telling the school, students who are bullied can get support and help to make things better.

Show proof of what happened. Giving evidence of cyberbullying to the school helps them take the right actions against the bullies and support the victims. Schools need accurate information to deal with bad behavior and punish those who are responsible. Victims should work together with the school and give proof of what happened so the school can handle it well and keep all students safe.

Shielding the Screen: Empowering Strategies Against Cyberbullying

Preventive Measures

Preventing cyberbullying as a parent involves proactive strategies to ensure your child's safety and well-being in the digital world. These strategies include:

- **Limit access to technology:**

Set boundaries on screen time and digital device usage to mitigate exposure to cyberbullying. Encourage alternative activities like outdoor play, hobbies, or family time without screens. Designate specific areas in the home as technology-free zones to promote face-to-face interactions and reduce reliance on digital devices.

- **Consider monitoring your child's social media use:**

Stay vigilant about your child's online presence to detect signs of cyberbullying early. Utilize monitoring tools or parental controls to oversee their social media interactions while respecting their privacy. Keep communication lines open to discuss any concerns or alarming behavior observed during monitoring.

- **Know what sites your child uses:**

Take the time to familiarize yourself with the platforms and websites your child frequents online. Understand the features, privacy settings, and potential risks associated with each platform to better guide and protect your child's online experience. Stay informed about emerging trends and popular apps to address evolving digital threats.

- **Be part of your kids' online world:**

Make sure you talk openly with your kid about what they do online, what they like, and who they talk to. Show that you really care about what they're doing on the internet and make it easy for them to tell you if something's bothering them or if they run into any problems online. Building trust and respect helps keep the conversation going about staying safe online.

- **Get to know your children's online friends:**

Encourage your child to introduce you to their online friends and acquaintances. Build rapport with their online community to gain insight into their social interactions and identify potential risks or warning signs of cyberbullying. Foster a sense of accountability and encourage transparency in online relationships.

- **Discuss with kids if bullying is suspected:**

When you talk to your child about cyberbullying, be kind and understanding. Make sure they feel safe telling you how they feel without worrying about being judged. Listen carefully to what they say and let them know their feelings are important. Help them come up with ways to deal with cyberbullying together.

- **Block the bully:**

Empower your child with the tools and knowledge to block or unfriend individuals engaging in bullying behavior online. Teach them how to set boundaries and assertively address harassment or intimidation. Reinforce the importance of prioritizing their mental and emotional well-being by taking proactive steps to protect themselves from further harm.

- **Differentiate tattling from reporting for kids:**

Educate your child on the distinction between tattling (reporting minor issues for personal gain) and reporting (seeking assistance to address serious concerns or threats). Foster a culture of accountability and encourage responsible reporting of cyberbullying incidents to trusted adults or authorities. Empower your child to advocate for their safety and the safety of others in their online community.

- **Put it in writing:**

Establish clear guidelines and expectations regarding online behavior and safety through a family agreement or contract. Outline rules for responsible technology use, consequences for violating guidelines, and procedures for reporting cyberbullying incidents. Regularly review and revise the agreement to accommodate your child's growth and evolving digital habits while reinforcing the importance of online safety.

Promoting Empathy and Respect

Promoting online empathy and respect means creating an environment where kindness and understanding are valued. It's crucial to remember that behind every screen is a real person with feelings. Teaching teens to think critically about their online actions helps them grasp the impact of their words and behavior.

- **Be respectful—and expect respect:**

When you're online, you should act just like you would in real life—with kindness and understanding. That means avoiding saying mean things, making fun of others, or being a cyberbully. When you treat people nicely online, it helps make the internet a better place where everyone can get along. Being respectful when you talk to others online helps them feel understood and cared for. It also builds trust and makes the online world a safer and happier place for everyone. So, remember to be nice and considerate when you're chatting online, just like you would if you were talking face-to-face.

- **Protect your reputation:**

Your online presence is like your virtual identity. Everything you do or say online, such as posting, commenting, or sharing, adds up to how people see you. So, it's really important to be careful about what you share because it can affect how others perceive you. Making sure you only share things that reflect your values and make you look good helps build a positive image online. When you protect your reputation on the internet, you're also protecting your honesty and trustworthiness, which can affect the opportunities you have in your personal and professional life later on.

- **Protect your privacy:**

In the digital age, safeguarding personal information is paramount. Teens should understand the importance of keeping sensitive details confidential, such as their address, phone number, or private photos. Sharing such information online can leave them vulnerable to various risks, including identity theft, cyberstalking, or online harassment. Respecting one's privacy and that of others creates a safer online environment where individuals feel secure and confident in their interactions. By exercising caution and discretion with personal information, teens can mitigate the potential for harm and maintain control over their online identities.

- **Think critically:**

Since there's so much information online, you need to act carefully about what you're reading or watching. It's good to teach teens to ask questions about where the info is coming from, look at different sides of a story, and check if what they're seeing is actually true. When you can think critically, it helps you figure out what's reliable and what's not, like spotting lies or unfair ideas. By teaching teens to think critically, we're giving them the skills they need to make smart choices, be careful about what they see online, and add positive stuff to online conversations.

Supporting Victims

Supporting victims of cyberbullying involves providing emotional support, guidance, and practical assistance to help them cope with and address the situation effectively. The following are the different ways you can support the victim:

- **Offer comfort and support:**

When someone is being cyberbullied, you have to be there for them. Letting them know they're not alone and that you're there to listen and help can make a big difference. It's important to show that you understand how they're feeling and that it's okay to feel that way. By being a good listener and showing you care, you give them a safe place to talk about what's happening without worrying about being judged.

- **Let your child know that it's not their fault:**

Victims of cyberbullying often internalize blame and guilt, believing that they somehow caused or deserve the harassment. Reassuring them that they are not at fault is essential in helping them overcome these feelings of self-blame. Emphasize that the responsibility lies with the perpetrator of the cyberbullying and that the victim should not feel responsible for the actions of others. By shifting the focus away from self-blame, you empower the victim to recognize their worth and seek support without hesitation.

- **Make sure your child feels safe:**

When dealing with cyberbullying, the most important thing is to make sure the person being bullied feels safe both online and in their feelings. You can talk about ways to stay safe, like changing privacy settings on social media, blocking or reporting the bully, and not talking to people you don't know online. It's really important to stress the importance of keeping personal info private and not giving the bully any attention. By giving practical tips on how to stay safe online, you help the person being bullied feel more in control and secure when they're online.

- **Encourage your child not to respond to cyberbullying:**

It's important to discourage the victim from responding to cyberbullying, as doing so can escalate the situation and provide the bully with further ammunition. Instead, encourage the victim to focus on seeking support and reporting the incident to appropriate authorities. Emphasize the importance of maintaining composure and not allowing the bully's actions to dictate their responses. By refraining from engaging with the bully, the victim can avoid perpetuating the cycle of harassment and instead take proactive steps towards resolution and support.

- **Notify the school:**

Informing the school administration or relevant authorities about cyberbullying incidents involving students from the same school is crucial. Schools typically have established protocols to address bullying cases effectively. By notifying the school, victims can access support services, and appropriate action can be taken to ensure their safety. School authorities can intervene, investigate the matter, and implement disciplinary measures if necessary. Additionally, informing the school creates awareness of the issue within the educational community, fostering a safer environment for all students.

- **Avoid contacting the bully's parents:**

While it may be tempting to directly approach the parents of the bully, it's often more productive to involve school officials or law enforcement agencies if required. Direct communication with the bully's parents might escalate tensions or lead to further conflict. School authorities are better equipped to handle such situations diplomatically and impartially. They can mediate discussions between involved parties and enforce consequences for the bully's behavior. Involving parents should ideally occur through formal channels with the assistance of school administrators to ensure a constructive resolution.

- **Keep records:**

Encouraging victims to document cyberbullying incidents is essential for several reasons. Keeping records, including screenshots of offensive messages or posts along with dates and times, provides tangible evidence of the harassment. These records can support the victim's case when reporting the bullying to school officials or law enforcement. Additionally, documenting the incidents helps victims track patterns of behavior and assess the severity of the situation. It also aids in identifying trends or recurring themes in the bullying, which can inform intervention strategies and preventive measures.

- **Get help:**

Getting help from experts like counselors, therapists, or support groups that know about cyberbullying is really important if you're going through it. These professionals give you a safe place to talk about your feelings and deal with what's happened to you. They help you figure out how to handle cyberbullying and give you back some control over your life. In counseling or therapy, you can learn ways to stay strong, stand up for yourself, and take care of yourself emotionally. And being in a support group can make you feel less alone because you're with other people who understand what you're going through.

Interactive Activity

Cyberbullying Awareness Quiz for Teenagers

Instructions: Answer the following questions to test your knowledge and awareness of cyberbullying. Choose the best answer for each question.

1. What is cyberbullying?

a) Physical altercation between students

b) Sending mean or hurtful messages online or posting embarrassing photos

c) Playing pranks on classmates during school hours

d) Ignoring someone intentionally in social situations

1. Which of the following is an example of cyberbullying?

a) Complimenting a friend's photo on social media

b) Sending a threatening message to someone online

c) Inviting friends to a group chat

d) Sharing a funny meme with classmates

   1. True or False: Cyberbullying only occurs through direct messages on social media platforms.

   2. What are some potential consequences of cyberbullying for the victim?

a) Increased self-esteem

b) Improved relationships with peers

c) Anxiety, depression, or suicidal thoughts

d) Enhanced social status

   1. What should you do if you witness cyberbullying?

a) Join in and support the bully

b) Report the incident to a trusted adult or authority figure

c) Ignore it and pretend it didn't happen

d) Laugh along with the bully to fit in

   1. True or False: It is important to keep cyberbullying incidents a secret and not tell anyone about them.

   2. How can you protect yourself from cyberbullying?

a) Sharing personal information online

b) Accepting friend requests from strangers

c) Using strong and unique passwords for your accounts

d) Responding aggressively to hurtful messages

1. What should you do if you are being cyberbullied?

a) Retaliate with mean messages

b) Keep it to yourself and try to handle it alone

c) Seek help from a trusted adult or counselor

d) Delete your social media accounts

1. Which of the following behaviors is NOT a form of cyberbullying?

a) Spreading rumors or gossip online

b) Excluding someone from a group chat

c) Posting positive comments on a friend's photo

d) Sending threatening or harassing messages

1. True or False: Cyberbullying can have serious legal consequences for the perpetrator.

Scoring:

- 1 point for each correct answer
- Total possible points: 10

Interpretation:

- 0-3 points: Low Awareness - Consider learning more about cyberbullying and its impacts.

- 4-7 points: Moderate Awareness - You have a basic understanding of cyberbullying, but there's room for improvement.

- 8-10 points: High Awareness - Well done! You have a strong awareness of cyberbullying and how to address it.

In conclusion, cyberbullying is a significant concern impacting numerous teenagers today. It's crucial to grasp what cyberbullying entails, including various forms like sending hurtful messages or spreading rumors online. The repercussions of cyberbullying on mental well-being can be severe, causing emotions such as sadness, depression, and even thoughts of self-harm. It's distressing to note that many victims endure lasting effects that hinder their learning and sense of security. To counter cyberbullying, you need to promptly report incidents and take preventive measures. This may involve reducing access to technology, fostering empathy and kindness online, and offering support to those who are targeted. Collaborative efforts to tackle cyberbullying can pave the way for a safer and more positive online space for everyone.

In the next chapter, you will gain a comprehensive understanding of teen depression, including its signs, causes, and the impact of social media, equipped with practical strategies to recognize, support, and empower teenagers struggling with depression.

Shadows of the Mind: Challenging Teen Depression

A human being can survive almost anything as long as she
sees the end in sight. But depression is so insidious, and it
compounds daily, that it's impossible to ever see the end. –
Elizabeth Wurtzel

If you've ever wondered whether you or someone you know might be experiencing depression but weren't sure if what you observed or felt fit the typical criteria, you're not alone. Depression is indeed intricate, much like each individual's unique experiences and personality.

According to Mental Health America, depressive disorders comprise a range of mood disorders characterized by prolonged periods of low mood that significantly disrupt a person's ability to find joy in life. While prevalent in the United States, depressive disorders do not adhere to a one-size-fits-all model, which can make navigating them challenging. There exist multiple variations of depression, each with its own distinct causes, symptoms, and severity levels.

Unveiling the Darkness: Understanding Teen Depression

Depression is a significant medical condition that has a profound impact on a person's emotions, thoughts, and behaviors. It's quite prevalent, affecting many individuals worldwide. The disorder manifests as persistent feelings of sadness and a lack of interest in activities that used to bring joy. Alongside these emotional symptoms, depression can also lead to various physical health issues.

Dealing with depression can be incredibly difficult because it can severely disrupt everyday life. It can make it hard to perform well at work and maintain healthy relationships with others. Even simple tasks that were once easy to handle may suddenly feel overwhelming, and this can greatly reduce a person's overall productivity.

There are five most common types of depressive disorders among teens and young adults, and they include:

Major Depressive Disorder (MDD)

This one is commonly referred to as *clinical depression*, stands as one of the prevalent mental health conditions in the United States. According to a comprehensive report released by the National Institutes of Mental Health in 2020, nearly 8% of U.S. adults grapple with this disorder. Interestingly, the burden of MDD appears to weigh heaviest on young adults, particularly those aged between 18 and 25 years.

However, the reach of this condition extends beyond adulthood, affecting approximately 17%—equivalent to 4.1 million—adolescents aged 12 to 17 years (Bachert, 2022).

Despite the alarming prevalence rates, major depressive disorder in children and adolescents often flies under the radar of diagnosis and treatment. This oversight can have far-reaching consequences, negatively impacting academic performance, social interactions, and even escalating the risk of suicidal behaviors among affected individuals.

Major depression manifests differently from person to person, but it invariably brings forth overwhelming symptoms that disrupt one's emotional state, functional capabilities, and overall quality of life. To merit an official diagnosis of major depression, an individual must exhibit five or more of the following symptoms consistently for at least two weeks:

- Persistent feelings of sadness or anxiety
- Irritability
- Loss of interest in hobbies and activities
- Feelings of hopelessness
- Feelings of guilt, worthlessness, or helplessness
- Restlessness
- Fatigue
- Slowed movement or speech

- Difficulty concentrating, remembering, or making decisions

- Sleep disturbances

- Changes in appetite or weight

- Suicidal thoughts

While this might seem like an exhaustive list, it's crucial to note that not every individual grappling with major depression will experience all these symptoms. However, the presence of a significant subset of these symptoms for a sustained period serves as a hallmark of this debilitating condition.

Persistent Depressive Disorder (PDD)

It is also known as *dysthymia*, is a form of depression characterized by prolonged periods of low mood and other associated symptoms. In teenagers, PDD is diagnosed when symptoms persist for more than one year, while in adults, it extends beyond two years. Though it's often considered milder than major depression, its long-lasting nature can still have significant impacts on a person's life if left untreated.

Identifying signs of PDD is crucial for timely intervention. Individuals with PDD may exhibit a range of symptoms, including frequent irritability, persistent feelings of low self-esteem, fatigue, difficulty in making decisions, and a pervasive sense of hopelessness. Additionally, changes in eating and sleeping habits might also be noticeable indicators of PDD.

One of the key distinguishing factors of PDD is the persistence of symptoms. Unlike episodic depressive episodes, where symptoms might come and go, individuals with PDD experience these symptoms for most of the day, nearly every day, for an extended period. This chronicity is a hallmark feature of PDD and helps differentiate it from other forms of depression.

Addressing PDD requires a holistic strategy, which could encompass psychotherapy, medication, adjustments in lifestyle, and leading to social support. Through accessing suitable treatment options, individuals grappling with PDD can acquire skills to cope with their symptoms and enhance their well-being. Timely recognition and action are pivotal in averting the potential repercussions of unaddressed PDD, especially in adolescents and young adults who are in the process of developing vital coping mechanisms and self-understanding.

Bipolar disorder

Bipolar disorder is a mental health condition distinguished by significant mood swings, which can vary from severe depression to intense episodes of mania. These mood swings can really mess with how someone thinks, feels, and acts. There are different types of bipolar disorder, but they all involve feeling really down and then getting really high.

During a depressive episode, individuals may experience sadness, loss of interest, sleep and appetite disturbances, fatigue, and difficulty concentrating. But when they're in a manic episode, it's like they have tons of energy, feel super happy, can't stop thinking quickly, and might do things without thinking about the consequences.

Bipolar disorder usually starts when people are in their late teens or early twenties, but some might have symptoms earlier. Sometimes, it takes a long time to get diagnosed, like 6-8 years, especially in younger people. This can make it tough to manage the condition properly. People with bipolar disorder not only deal with mental health problems but also have a higher chance of having other health issues like diabetes or heart problems. So, it's essential for them to get the right support and treatment.

Premenstrual Dysphoric Disorder (PMDD)

PMDD is a highly incapacitating condition that impacts women during the days leading up to their menstrual cycle. While many women undergo some level of discomfort or mood alterations before menstruation, PMDD represents a severe manifestation of premenstrual syndrome (PMS), marked by intense emotional and physical symptoms. Unlike typical PMS, which may entail mood swings and irritability, PMDD stands out due to its extreme severity and its significant impact on daily functioning. Although it's estimated that approximately 40% of women experience some form of PMS, only a small percentage, approximately 3-5%, receive a diagnosis of PMDD. This condition can deeply affect a woman's mental well-being, leading to severe anxiety, depression, and in severe cases, even suicidal ideation (Bachert, 2022).

The symptoms of PMDD can cause significant distress and have wide-reaching effects on a woman's life. They can impair her performance at work, disrupt her relationships, impact her sexual activity, and challenge her ability to fulfill her responsibilities at home. Although the severity of these symptoms may vary from one menstrual cycle to another, they typically begin approximately six days before menstruation and diminish within two or three days after its onset. In order to be diagnosed with PMDD, a woman must experience these symptoms consistently for at least two consecutive menstrual cycles. This criterion is important for distinguishing PMDD from temporary mood changes or discomfort associated with normal menstrual cycles.

Seasonal Affective Disorder (SAD)

SAD is a type of depression that hits during certain times of the year, usually in fall and winter. It gets better as spring and summer roll in. While it's normal to feel a bit down with the changing seasons, SAD is more serious and keeps coming back, affecting how you eat, sleep, and feel.

It usually starts when you're a young adult and affects about 5% of adults in the US. Interestingly, it's more common in women, with about 75% of those affected being female. SAD symptoms last for about 4-5 months during the affected season and look a lot like major depression (Bachert, 2022).

In the winter, when SAD is most common, you might sleep a lot, eat more than usual, gain weight, and want to be alone more often. These symptoms really mess with how you feel and function.

In contrast, some people get SAD in spring and summer, which is less common. Symptoms for this type include trouble sleeping, not feeling hungry, losing weight, feeling restless, and being more anxious. In rare cases, some people might even get aggressive.

The fact that SAD comes and goes with the seasons shows how much the environment affects our mood. Treating SAD usually involves a mix of therapies like light therapy, counseling, medication, and making lifestyle changes to feel better all year round.

However, despite their differences, all forms of depression share a common thread. Any sign or symptom of depression represents a significant mental health condition capable of impacting a teen's quality of life in both the short and long term. These signs include:

- Lack of interest or motivation

- Complaints of physical discomforts such as headaches, stomachaches, back pain, or fatigue

- Challenges with focus or concentration

- Difficulty in decision-making

- Experiencing excessive or inappropriate feelings of guilt

- Engaging in irresponsible behaviors, like neglecting responsibilities, tardiness, or absenteeism from school

- Loss of appetite or engaging in binge eating leading to significant changes in weight

- Memory difficulties

- Fixation on thoughts of death or dying

- Demonstrating rebellious conduct

- Feelings of sadness, anxiousness, or hopelessness

- Disturbed sleep patterns, staying awake at night and sleeping during the day

- Sudden decline in academic performance

- Involvement in substance abuse or risky sexual behavior

- Withdrawal from social interactions and friendships

- Sensation of helplessness

- Unexplained bouts of crying

- High sensitivity to rejection or perceived failure

Teen depression rates are concerning. Between 3-9% of teenagers experience depression at any given time, and by the end of adolescence, up to 20% of teenagers report having experienced depression at some point in their lives (Goyal et al., 2009).

The impact of depression on academic performance is notable. Depressed teens often struggle to concentrate, have low motivation, and experience difficulty completing assignments or studying, which can lead to a decline in grades and academic achievement. This can perpetuate a cycle of stress and further exacerbate their depressive symptoms.

Socially, depression can strain relationships with peers and family members. Teenagers may withdraw from social activities, experience conflicts with friends, or isolate themselves, leading to feelings of loneliness and alienation. Additionally, depressed teens may engage in risky behaviors or substance abuse as a way to cope, further complicating their social interactions and well-being.

Tracing the Roots: Exploring the Causes of Adolescent Depression

Depression can be caused by several factors. These factors can be either biological, physiological, or environmental.

Biological Factors

These include:

- **Genetics**:

Genetics play a significant role in the development of depression. Research suggests that individuals with a family history of depression are more likely to experience depression themselves. This doesn't mean that depression is entirely predetermined by genetics, but it does indicate a predisposition. Certain genes may influence how the brain regulates mood and stress responses, making some individuals more susceptible to depression than others.

- **Hormones**:

Hormones, which are chemical messengers in the body, can also influence mood and mental health. During adolescence, hormonal changes are particularly prominent as the body undergoes significant development. Fluctuations in hormones, such as cortisol (the stress hormone), estrogen, progesterone, and testosterone, can impact mood regulation. For example, imbalances in these hormones may contribute to mood swings, irritability, and feelings of sadness or anxiety, all of which are common symptoms of depression in teens.

- **Brain chemicals**:

The brain relies on various neurotransmitters, or brain chemicals, to regulate mood, emotions, and behavior. Serotonin, dopamine, and norepinephrine are among the neurotransmitters implicated in depression. These chemicals help transmit signals between nerve cells and are involved in regulating mood, sleep, appetite, and stress responses. In individuals with depression, there may be imbalances or dysregulation in these neurotransmitter systems. For instance, low levels of serotonin are often associated with feelings of sadness and low mood, while disruptions in dopamine pathways can affect motivation and pleasure. These chemical imbalances can contribute to the onset and persistence of depressive symptoms in teens.

Psychological Factor

These factors are as follows:

- **Chronic stress**:

Teens deal with a lot of things that stress them out, like schoolwork, what others expect from them, fights at home, or problems with friends. When stress sticks around for a long time and feels like too much to handle, it can mess with how they feel and make them more likely to get depressed. Feeling constantly overwhelmed or like they can't handle what's happening can lead to feeling down and having other signs of depression.

- **History of trauma**:

Going through trauma when you're a kid or teenager can really mess with your head. It can make you feel scared, helpless, and really upset. These feelings from the trauma can stick with you and might even make you depressed when you're older.

- **Pessimism**:

If teenagers always see things in a bad way or expect the worst, they might be more likely to get depressed. When they keep thinking negatively, it can mess up how they see what's really happening and make it hard for them to feel hopeful or think things will get better. This can make them feel really sad and like there's no way out of it.

- **Self-doubt**:

Adolescents who struggle with self-doubt or low confidence may be at a higher risk of depression. Constantly questioning their abilities, worth, or value can undermine their self-esteem and contribute to feelings of inadequacy or unworthiness. These negative self-perceptions can fuel depressive symptoms and make it challenging for teenagers to maintain a positive sense of self.

- **Low self-esteem**:

When teenagers feel really bad about themselves, it can lead to depression. They might feel like nobody cares about them, like they're not good at anything, or like they don't deserve to be happy. These thoughts make them feel even worse, and it becomes a cycle. Teens with low self-esteem might constantly criticize themselves, compare themselves to others in a bad way, and find it hard to make friends.

- **Moodiness**:

Mood swings and fluctuations in emotions are common during adolescence due to hormonal changes and developmental transitions. However, persistent moodiness or extreme fluctuations in mood may indicate underlying emotional distress. Teenagers who experience frequent and intense mood swings may be more vulnerable to depression, especially if they struggle to regulate their emotions effectively.

- **Highly sensitive**:

Some teenagers are highly sensitive to their surroundings, emotions, and interpersonal dynamics. While sensitivity can be a valuable trait, it can also make individuals more susceptible to experiencing emotional distress. High levels of sensitivity may amplify the impact of stressors, criticism, or negative experiences, making teenagers more prone to developing depressive symptoms.

Environmental Influences

Such factors include the following:

- **Family environment:**

Family dynamics and relationships can greatly impact adolescent mental health. Issues such as parental conflict, divorce, neglect, or abuse can create an environment of stress and instability, contributing to feelings of sadness, insecurity, and low self-esteem in adolescents. Also, a lack of emotional support or healthy communication within the family can hinder coping mechanisms and exacerbate depressive symptoms.

- **Peer relationships:**

Teens hang out a lot with their friends, and how good these friendships are can affect how they feel. Bullying, being left out, or feeling pressure to do risky things because of friends can make teens feel really lonely, worthless, or worried. This can make them more likely to feel depressed. Also, if they don't have good friends who support them or feel like they fit in, it can make them feel even more alone and disconnected.

- **Academic pressure:**

School can be a big source of stress for teenagers. They often feel pressure from parents, teachers, and society to do well. This, along with tough schoolwork and worrying about how they're doing, can make them feel like they're not good enough. If they struggle in school or worry a lot about failing, it can make them feel even worse about themselves. This can lead to feeling really down, especially if they think not doing well in school means they're failing as a person.

- **Social media and technology:**

The use of social media and digital gadgets by teens has brought in new factors that can affect mental health. Spending too much time on social media can make teens compare themselves to others unrealistically, face cyberbullying, and feel like they're not good enough or missing out on things. Seeing perfect pictures and lifestyles on social media all the time can make teens feel like their own lives aren't good enough and make them feel bad about themselves.

- **Traumatic experiences:**

When teenagers experience really tough things like abuse, violence, losing someone they love, or going through natural disasters, it can make them more likely to feel depressed. Trauma messes up how they usually handle tough situations, which can lead to feeling sad, anxious, or even getting PTSD. If they don't deal with the tough stuff they went through, it can show up as bad behaviors or having a hard time controlling their emotions, making the depression worse.

Extending a Lifeline: Supporting Teens Through Depression

Suicide Warnings

Severely depressed teens, especially those with substance abuse issues, frequently contemplate, discuss, or attempt suicide, and an alarming number succeed. Therefore, it's crucial to take any signs of suicidal thoughts or actions seriously, as they indicate a plea for help from your teenager. These signs include:

- Mentioning or joking about suicide.

- Expressing thoughts such as, "Life isn't worth living," "I wish I could just disappear," or "There's no hope for me."

- Showing fascination with death or portraying it romantically ("Maybe if I were gone, people would care more").

- Creating written works like stories or poems centered on death, dying, or suicide.

- Engaging in risky behaviors or experiencing frequent accidents resulting in harm.

- Giving away valued possessions.

- Bidding farewell to loved ones as if it were final.

- Seeking access to weapons, medication, or other means for self-harm.

It's shocking to know that suicide is the third leading cause of death among young people aged 15 to 24. This shows how serious the problem is and how urgent it is to do something about it. Depression is a big factor that increases the risk of suicide. Studies say that if someone is depressed, they're 14 times more likely to try to end their life. This tells us how crucial it is to spot and deal with mental health problems early on (Suicide, 2018).

What's really sad is that more than half of young people who are dealing with depression will try to kill themselves. And out of those, over 7% will actually succeed (Education-Teen Suicide, n.d.). These numbers remind us how much mental health issues can affect young lives and why it's so important to do something about it.

To help teenagers dealing with these issues, there are a few things you can do. First, pay close attention to them; watch how they act, listen to what they say, and try to understand how they feel. Talking to them in a kind and open way can help them feel safe to share their thoughts and feelings with you.

If you notice any signs that they're struggling, don't wait; get them help from professionals like counselors or therapists right away. This can make a big difference in getting them the support they need to feel better.

How to Help a Teenager With Depression

If you want to help your teen with depression, you do not have to go all in and confront them. You can follow the following tips.

- **Learn about depression**

When someone we care about, like a teenager, is diagnosed with depression, it's crucial to learn about it ourselves. This helps us understand what they're dealing with and how we can support them better. Teens themselves can tell us a lot about how they feel. We should be there to listen when they want to talk about what's troubling them. Encouraging them to open up can make a big difference.

- **Help the teen understand depression**

When we talk to a teenager about depression, we can help them understand what's going on with their feelings and why it's important to get help. We can tell them that depression is quite common, so they don't feel like they're the only one going through it.

Sometimes, comparing depression to a physical illness like diabetes can make it easier for them to understand. We can say something like, "Depression is a mental illness, similar to how the flu or other sicknesses can make you feel tired or give you a headache. It can also affect your emotions, making you feel sad, lonely, frustrated, angry, or scared."

This helps them see that depression is a real thing that needs treatment, just like any other illness.

- **Let them know what to expect**

When teenagers understand what their treatment involves and have positive expectations about it, they're more likely to follow through with it. It can be scary not knowing what's going to happen, so it's good to explain what their treatment plan might be like and why it's important for them to do their part.

For example, we can say, "Taking your medicine every day and going to therapy once a week is important to help you feel better. In therapy, you can talk privately about how you're feeling. The medicine might make you feel tired or dizzy at first, but that should get better soon. That's why you'll see the doctor once a month. They'll ask how the medicine is affecting you and make sure it's helping." This way, they know what to expect and why it's essential for their recovery.

- **Give them some control**

Teenagers might be more willing to follow their treatment plan if they feel involved in the decision-making process. When they have a sense of control, it helps them grow and learn how to make good choices for themselves.

While it's not possible for teens to completely plan their treatment, letting them make some small decisions can make a big difference. For instance, we can ask them, "Your therapist wants to see you every week. What day works best for you? Would you prefer going right after school or after dinner?" This way, they feel like they have a say in their treatment, which can make them more likely to stick with it.

- **Leveraging active listening**

Think back to when your child used to share everything with you, from their wildest dreams to their most random thoughts. Now that they're a teenager, they might not be as open.

When you're trying to connect with them, remember that sometimes saying less can be more effective. By listening more than you talk, you might help a guarded teen feel more comfortable opening up.

Instead of bombarding them with questions, focus on being approachable and creating an environment where they feel safe to talk. Pay attention to the little things they do share, and ask about those. These small details could mean a lot to your teen.

Practicing active listening can also help build trust with your teen. That way, if they ever need to talk about more sensitive topics, like symptoms of depression, they'll feel more comfortable coming to you.

- **Validate their experience**

Whether your teen is dealing with depression or not, they're facing a lot of new challenges in their social life, physical changes, academics, and emotions. It's a really stressful time for them.

One thing to avoid is belittling or dismissing what they're going through or trying to convince them that it's not a big deal. Doing this can make them less likely to open up to you in the future.

As a parent, you might have always been there to solve your child's problems, but as they become more independent teenagers, it's important to give them space to figure things out on their own.

When your teen does come to you with their problems or disappointments, try to understand how they're feeling. This is a time for empathy, not necessarily for giving advice unless they ask for it. Just being there to listen and support them can make a big difference.

- **Encourage supportive relationships**

Building supportive relationships is really important, especially for teenagers who are dealing with depression. Depression can make them want to be alone and pull away from friends and family, which can make them feel even more sad and lonely.

But having just one friend or supportive adult to talk to can make a big difference. We can be that person by letting them know we're here for them anytime they need to talk. We can also encourage them to reach out to friends and share their feelings.

For example, we could say, "I'm always here if you need someone to talk to. It's also good to talk to your friends. Having people who care about you and cheer you up is really important. Sharing how you feel can make tough times a bit easier. Is there a friend you feel comfortable talking to?"

It's also important to help them stick to healthy routines, like taking their medication and eating well. Encouraging them to do things that make them feel better, and making sure their home is a safe and comforting place, can also be really helpful.

- **Address myths**

Teens might have heard negative things about mental illness or felt the social stigma around it. It's important to talk to them about this so they don't feel like they have to keep their depression a secret or be ashamed of it.

We can remind them that some people might not understand or might have the wrong ideas about depression, but that doesn't mean they should feel embarrassed. They have the choice to tell others about their diagnosis, but they don't have to hide it.

We should also help them keep up with positive routines like taking their medication and eating well. Encouraging them to do things that make them feel good and making sure their home is a safe and comforting place can also make a big difference.

Common Treatment

Getting help from a professional for teenagers dealing with depression is really important. It means they'll get the right kind of help and advice to handle what they're going through. What are the common types of treatment for depression?

1. **Cognitive Behavioral Therapy (CBT)**: This therapy is all about finding and fixing the negative thoughts and behaviors that make depression worse. It helps teenagers develop coping strategies and problem-solving skills to deal with their symptoms.

2. **Interpersonal Psychotherapy for Adolescents (IPT-A)**: IPT-A concentrates on improving communication and relationships to alleviate depression symptoms. It helps teenagers address interpersonal issues and conflicts that may be contributing to their depression, such as family problems or social difficulties.

3. **Medications**: Doctors sometimes give antidepressant pills to teenagers who are feeling really down. These pills help fix the balance of chemicals in the brain, which can make them feel better and lessen the symptoms of depression. There are different kinds of these pills, like SSRIs and SNRIs, which do similar things to help improve mood.

All these treatments can help teenagers deal with and beat depression, but which one is best depends on what each person needs. It's really important for teens to talk with mental health experts to figure out the right treatment plan for them.

Interactive Element

PHQ-9

Below are the questions designed to help identify symptoms of depression in teenagers. Please follow the instructions carefully to administer and score the test accurately. If a teen scores high on this questionnaire, it is essential to seek professional support for proper guidance and diagnosis.

Instructions:

1. Provide a comfortable and confidential environment for the teen to answer the questions.

2. Read each question aloud and ask the teen to respond honestly based on how they have been feeling over the past two weeks.

3. For each question, ask the teen to select the response that best reflects their experience:

    ○ 0: Not at all

    ○ 1: Several days

    ○ 2: More than half the days

    ○ 3: Nearly every day

4. Add up the scores for all nine questions to obtain the total score.

5. Interpret the results based on the scoring guide provided.

Scoring Guide:

- 0-4: Minimal depression symptoms

- 5-9: Mild depression symptoms

- 10-14: Moderate depression symptoms

- 15-19: Moderately severe depression symptoms

- 20-27: Severe depression symptoms

Questionnaire

Over the past two weeks:

1. How often have you been bothered by little interest or pleasure in doing things?

    ○ 0: Not at all

- 1: Several days

- 2: More than half the days

- 3: Nearly every day

2. How often have you been bothered by feeling down, depressed, or hopeless?

3. How often have you been bothered by trouble falling or staying asleep, or sleeping too much?

4. How often have you been bothered by feeling tired or having little energy?

5. How often have you been bothered by poor appetite or overeating?

6. How often have you been bothered by feeling bad about yourself, or how often have you felt like you are a failure or have let yourself or your family down?

7. How often do you find it hard to focus on things, like reading or watching TV?

8. Have you ever felt like you were moving or talking really slowly to the point where others might have noticed? Or maybe you've been the opposite, feeling super restless and unable to stay still, constantly moving around more than usual?

9. How many times have you felt like life would be easier if you weren't around or thought about hurting yourself?

Important Note: If the total score indicates moderate to severe depression symptoms (10 or above), it is crucial to seek professional support for proper guidance and diagnosis. Remember, this questionnaire is a tool to start conversations and identify potential mental health concerns in teenagers. Professional assistance can provide comprehensive evaluation and appropriate treatment options.

To conclude, understanding teen depression is crucial for recognizing and addressing the challenges adolescents face in today's complex world. By defining depression and identifying its signs and symptoms, you become better equipped to support teenagers through their struggles. Recognizing the prevalence and impact of depression highlights the urgency of intervention and support. Exploring the root causes, including biological, psychological, and environmental factors, helps you understand the multifaceted nature of this condition. By extending a lifeline, offering support, and being vigilant for suicide warning signs, you can help save lives. Finally, knowing how to assist teenagers with depression, including seeking professional help and providing various forms of treatment, empowers you to make a difference in their journey toward healing and recovery.

In the next chapter, we will discuss about the importance of fostering open communication, trust, and proactive support strategies in building strong and resilient support networks for teenagers, empowering them to navigate the challenges of adolescence with confidence and well-being.

Anchoring Adolescence: Cultivating Resilient Support Networks

You have two hands. One to help yourself, and one to help others. –Audrey Hepburn

The Vitality of Candid Conversations

Creating Safe Spaces

Teens' mental health depends critically on creating spaces where they may freely express their ideas and feelings without worrying about being judged. Teens go through a lot of different emotions and experiences during their teenage years, which can be pretty tough. But when they have safe spaces to open up, it makes it easier for them to share their feelings and talk about what's going on. This kind of environment helps build trust and makes it more likely for teens to ask for help when they're struggling with things like feeling sad or anxious.

When teens feel like they're listened to and understood, it means their mental health problems are less likely to get worse. Plus, having a space where they won't be judged helps them grow emotionally and handle challenges better.

So, creating supportive places for teenagers is really important because it helps them feel understood and cared for, which is great for their mental health in the long run.

Active Listening Skills

Good communication between teens and parents needs something called *active listening*, which means really paying attention and understanding each other. Parents need to make sure teens feel like they're being heard and not judged.

To be an active listener for your teen, first, listen to them with intent by eliminating distractions and giving your undivided attention. Show that your teen is a priority by putting away phones and other diversions, engaging fully in conversations without multitasking.

Second, demonstrate interest by maintaining eye contact, using body language to convey attentiveness, and avoiding behaviors that signal disinterest.

Third, refrain from interrupting your teen; resist the urge to interject with advice or opinions, allowing them to express themselves fully and creating a safe space for open dialogue.

Fourth, practice mindful listening by being present in the moment without judgment, refraining from making assumptions, and validating your teen's experiences without immediately inserting parental perspectives.

Finally, ask thoughtful questions that deepen understanding and reflection, clarify points or feelings with compassionate inquiries, and guide conversations toward productive exploration and problem-solving, empowering your teen to find their own solutions.

Encouraging Openness

Initiating meaningful conversations with your teen can be challenging but essential for building a strong relationship based on trust and communication. Teens face various pressures and need parental support, making it crucial to connect authentically and understand their needs and interests. Here are strategies to start meaningful conversations and demonstrate support:

- **Use Positive and Encouraging Words:**

In guiding your teen through challenges, employ positive language to instill motivation and support. Reinforce their confidence and self-belief with affirming phrases such as, "You're doing great," or "I'm proud of you." These simple yet powerful words can uplift their spirits and encourage them to persevere through difficult times.

- **Create a Safe Space for Expression:**

Encourage your teen to share their feelings by fostering a comfortable environment where openness is embraced. Lead by example by sharing your own emotions and experiences, thereby building trust and promoting genuine communication.

- **Demonstrate Genuine Interest:**

Listen actively to your teen's thoughts and concerns, displaying genuine engagement through attentive body language and eye contact. Offer assistance and support without judgment, validating their feelings and experiences.

- **Empathize and Understand Their Perspective:**

Strive to see things from your teen's viewpoint, recognizing the unique challenges they face. Approach conversations with empathy and understanding, fostering mutual respect and effective communication.

- **Engage With Their Interests and Activities:**

Initiate conversations about topics and activities that interest your teen, demonstrating your curiosity and support. Spend quality time together participating in their hobbies or interests, fostering a sense of connection and rapport.

- **Support Rather Than Criticize:**

Provide guidance and encouragement without resorting to criticism, respecting your teen's autonomy and decisions. Offer assistance when needed, allowing them to seek guidance without fear of judgment.

- **Ask Meaningful Questions:**

Prompt deeper conversations by asking open-ended questions that encourage reflection and discussion. Listen attentively without offering unsolicited advice, allowing your teen to express themselves freely. By asking meaningful questions, you promote introspection and understanding within your relationship.

- **Respect Their Boundaries and Timing:**

Recognize and respect your teen's need for space and privacy, refraining from pressuring them to share when they're not ready. Be patient and understanding, demonstrating consistent support and availability for conversations when they arise.

- **Be Mindful of What They're Going Through:**

Approach conversations with sensitivity, acknowledging your teen's struggles and challenges with compassion. Offer support and encouragement rather than judgment or blame, demonstrating your unwavering commitment to their well-being. By being mindful of their experiences, you show them that they are not alone in their journey.

- **Encourage Independence and Decision-Making:**

Empower your teen to make their own decisions and navigate challenges autonomously. Offer guidance and assistance when needed, allowing them to learn and grow from their experiences. By fostering independence, you instill confidence and resilience in your teen.

- **Lead by Example:**

Model healthy communication and emotional expression in your interactions with your teen, setting a positive example for effective communication. Demonstrate empathy, respect, and understanding, reinforcing the importance of mutual respect and openness.

- **Celebrate Their Achievements and Efforts:**

Recognize and celebrate your teen's accomplishments and efforts, no matter how small. Show appreciation for their hard work and perseverance, reinforcing their sense of self-worth and confidence.

Establishing Trust: The Bedrock of Support

Consistency and Reliability

As a caregiver, being consistent in what you say and do is really important when dealing with teenagers. When you're consistent, it shows that you're reliable and trustworthy, which helps build a strong bond with the teens you're taking care of. They feel more secure and supported knowing they can count on you. But if you're not consistent, it can make them unsure and doubtful, which can strain your relationship.

So, by being consistent, like showing up when you say you will, listening to them, and being there to help, you're showing that you respect and care about them. This consistency helps them understand how much you value them, which makes your relationship even stronger as time goes on.

Honesty and Transparency

It's really important to be honest and open with teens to build a strong relationship based on trust. When you're honest, it shows them that you're open to hearing what they have to say too. This makes them feel comfortable sharing their thoughts and feelings with you because they know you'll be straight with them.

Being transparent, especially about tough topics, helps you talk about more complicated things with teens. When teens see that you're not afraid to talk about tough topics, they're more likely to have meaningful conversations with you. This helps them understand things better and learn how to think critically and solve problems.

Being truthful and open helps to create a solid trust between you and teens. When they know they can trust you to tell the truth, they feel respected and important. This trust is the foundation of a good relationship built on respect and understanding.

Strategies to Build Trust

Building trust with teens takes time and effort, but it's super important for a good relationship. When you have trust, you can talk openly and understand each other better. But if you mess up or don't pay attention, trust can disappear fast. To build trust with your teen, try these tips:

- **Listen first:** Teens want someone who will just listen without interrupting or judging. When you let them talk without jumping in with advice or opinions, it shows you care about what they have to say.

- **Support them:** Be interested in what your teen likes and what they're doing, even if it doesn't seem important to you. Celebrate their successes and encourage them when things don't go well. This helps them feel stronger and more confident.

- **Avoid punishment for openness:** If your teen opens up to you about something, try to be understanding and supportive, even if you don't agree with them. Punishing them for being honest might make them not want to talk to you in the future, which can hurt your relationship.

- **Show trust and belief:** Respect your teen's thoughts and feelings, even if they're different from yours. Let them know you trust them and believe in them. This helps build a relationship where you both feel respected and understood.

- **Respect their independence:** Treat your teen like they're growing up and can make their own choices. While it's important to guide them, giving them freedom in less important things helps them learn to be responsible and independent.

- **Acknowledge modern realities:** Understand that being a teenager today is different from when you were young, mainly because of things like social media and technology. Showing empathy for the challenges they face helps you connect better with your teen.

- **Relate through shared experiences:** Share stories from your own teenage years to bridge the gap between generations. Being open about your own struggles helps your teen feel like you understand what they're going through.

- **Maintain confidentiality:** Respect your teen's privacy by keeping what they tell you to yourself. Showing that you can be trusted with their secrets builds their confidence in you and strengthens your bond.

Respect for Autonomy

This is all about recognizing and honoring the teens' right to make their own decisions and take control of their actions. Just like adults, teens have their own thoughts and feelings that make them who they are. Respecting their freedom means recognizing they're unique and letting them express themselves however they want.

Giving teens the chance to decide things and own up to their choices is super important for them to grow. Whether it's big decisions or small ones, letting them choose teaches them about being responsible and facing the consequences of their actions. When they see what happens from their choices, they learn more about themselves and feel more confident about making decisions.

Respecting teens also means listening to what they have to say without judging them. Making a space where they can talk openly and share their thoughts without fear is key. When teens know they're being heard and understood, they're more likely to get involved and take part in making decisions.

Respecting teens' freedom also helps build trust between them and adults like parents or mentors. When teens feel their freedom is valued, they're more likely to trust the advice and help adults offer. This trust is the foundation for a strong and healthy relationship based on respect and understanding.

All in all, respecting teens' independence is really important for their growth and happiness. It helps them face the challenges of being a teenager with confidence, and it prepares them to become independent and responsible adults.

Connecting With Resources

You can give your child information, support, and direction by having a conversation with them about mental illness. It can be challenging for you to recognize mental illness in children. As a result, a large number of children who would benefit from therapy do not receive it. Understanding how to seek assistance and what to look out for is crucial.

So, if you need any assistance, you can try out the following:

- **Local Mental Health Clinics or Centers**: Communities offer mental health clinics with counseling, therapy, and psychiatric care. They specialize in caregiver support and provide personalized help. Find clinics online or contact your local health department for information.

- **Support Groups for Caregivers**: Support groups bring together caregivers facing similar challenges, providing a safe space to share experiences, gain insights, and receive emotional support. These groups may meet in-person or online, and they may focus on specific caregiving situations.

- **Online Resources and Forums**: Online platforms and forums can also be valuable resources for caregivers seeking support and information. Websites like Caregiver Action Network () or Psychology Today's therapist directory () can help caregivers connect with resources, professionals, and peer support online.

These resources can offer you valuable support, guidance, and encouragement as they navigate their caregiving journey.

Self-Care in Support: Nurturing Yourself Amidst Teen Challenges

Setting Boundaries

Taking care of yourself as a caregiver is crucial for your overall well-being. It's like being on an airplane; before helping others, you need to secure your own oxygen mask. Making sure you have boundaries and take time for self-care helps you stay strong physically, emotionally, and mentally. And when you're feeling good, you can be the best caregiver possible.

Setting boundaries means deciding what's okay and what's not in your relationships and interactions. You're literally drawing a line to show what you're comfortable with. When you set boundaries, you're not just looking out for yourself, but you're also showing others how to respect your needs and limits. So, remember to take care of yourself and set those boundaries; it's important for everyone involved.

Do you know how to set boundaries effectively? You can follow these tips:

1. **Begin with a reminder of your Love:** Start by reminding the teens that you care about them deeply. Let them know that setting boundaries is not about rejecting them but about taking care of yourself so you can continue to support them effectively.

2. **Explain and model limits:** Clearly explain what behaviors are acceptable and what are not. Show them through your actions how you uphold these limits. For example, if you need time alone to recharge, let them know and then take that time without feeling guilty.

3. **Communicate in a way teens will understand:** Use language that is clear and age-appropriate when

discussing boundaries with teens. Be patient and open to their questions or concerns. Help them understand that boundaries are a normal part of healthy relationships.

Remember, setting boundaries is not selfish; it's an essential part of self-care. By taking care of yourself, you're better able to care for others, including the teens in your life.

Seeking Support

When life gets tough, it's important to know that you're not alone. Talking to adults you trust, friends, or joining groups where people understand what you're going through can really help. Sharing your feelings lets you get them off your chest, get advice, and feel supported by others who have been through similar tough times.

Accepting your feelings means being okay with whatever emotions you're feeling whether they're good or bad. It's totally fine to feel sad, mad, or overwhelmed sometimes. When you accept your feelings, it helps you deal with them and move forward, which is really important for your emotional well-being.

If you're taking care of someone you love, it's crucial to get support for yourself too. Don't hesitate to ask other caregivers, family members, or professionals for help so you don't get overwhelmed. Remember, it's perfectly okay to reach out and ask for support when you need it.

Truly connecting with your partner means being there for them and understanding what they need. Listen to them, show that you care, and let them know that their feelings matter. When you have a strong bond with your loved one, it makes your relationship better and gives them the help they need.

Don't forget about yourself! Taking care of your own needs is super important for feeling good overall. Make time for things that make you happy, whether it's relaxing, doing things you enjoy, or just taking a breather. When you take care of yourself, you can be there more for others.

Sometimes, it's good to get extra help from your community. There are lots of services out there, like counseling or support groups, that can give you support and guidance when things get tough. It's totally okay to ask for help when you need it.

Practicing Self-Compassion

Looking after teens, whether you're a professional or a family member, can be exhausting. You need to take breaks and recharge yourself. If you're a family member looking after a teen, it can bring extra worries like money problems, arguments in the family, and feeling isolated from friends. Too much stress can lead to burnout, where you feel tired all the time, get easily annoyed, can't sleep well, gain weight, and feel really alone or hopeless. Burnout happens when stress piles up and starts causing problems in your body and mind, like headaches, tummy troubles, and getting sick more often. Taking care of yourself is super important to avoid burnout and keep yourself well.

You're doing your best and deserve to prioritize your own needs and health. It's like giving yourself a warm hug when things get tough, acknowledging that you're human and that it's okay to have ups and downs. Let's break down the steps of inner bonding, a process that helps you nurture self-compassion:

- **Accept that you are going to hurt, and own up to your emotions.** This step involves recognizing and accepting your emotions, even the painful ones. Instead of ignoring or pushing them away, you allow yourself to acknowledge and feel them. It's like giving yourself permission to say, "Hey, it's okay to feel this way. I'm here for you."

- **Move into the intent to learn.** Once you've acknowledged your feelings, the next step is to understand why you're feeling that way. This means being curious about your emotions and what they're trying to tell you. It's like asking yourself, "What can I learn from this? What is this feeling trying to teach me?"

- **Learn about your false beliefs.** Often, our negative emotions are rooted in false beliefs we hold about ourselves or the world around us. This step involves examining these beliefs and challenging their validity. It's like shining a light on the negative thoughts and asking yourself, "Is this really true? Or is it just a belief I've picked up along the way?"

- **Dialogue with your higher self.** Connecting with your higher self, or your inner wisdom, can provide guidance and support during challenging times. This step involves tuning into your intuition and seeking guidance from a place of love and compassion. It's like having a conversation with your wisest, most loving self, asking for advice and reassurance.

- **Take the loving action learned.** Take the loving action learned. Based on the insights gained from the previous steps, you can take proactive steps to take care of yourself and make yourself feel better. This might involve deciding what you're okay with and what you're not, doing things that make you feel good, or asking for help when you need it. It's like deciding to be nice to yourself and understanding that you deserve it.

- **Evaluate your action.** Finally, it's essential to reflect on the actions you've taken and their impact on your well-being. This step involves assessing what worked well and what could be improved upon for future self-care practices. It's like checking in with yourself regularly to see how you're feeling and adjusting your approach as needed.

In conclusion, taking care of teens' mental health is crucial, and it starts with creating safe spaces for them to express themselves without fear. Building trust through active listening and encouraging openness fosters healthy communication. Respecting their autonomy and setting boundaries show them they're valued. Seeking support, both for them and for yourself, is essential in navigating challenges. Practicing self-compassion is key; acknowledging emotions and taking steps to nurture well-being are vital. By prioritizing mental health and fostering supportive relationships, we empower teens to thrive emotionally and navigate life's challenges with resilience.

CONCLUSION

As we draw to a close, it's evident that understanding the evolving nature of teen mental health in the digital age is important. Throughout this book, we've been equipped with practical insights to effectively support and advocate for the well-being of our teenagers.

In our quest for understanding, we have gained invaluable insights into the different challenges faced by today's youth. From the perils of comparison culture to the prevalence of cyberbullying, from the complexities of body dysmorphia to the depths of teen depression, we have witnessed the myriad of ways in which the digital age intersects with mental well-being.

Yet, amidst these challenges, we have also discovered rays of hope and empowerment. We have unearthed practical strategies, actionable insights, and invaluable resources to support and advocate for the well-being of teenagers. We have learned the importance of digital literacy, fostering open communication and cultivating resilient support networks.

Our key takeaway from this journey is clear: Empowerment lies at the heart of effective support for teenagers. By equipping ourselves with knowledge, empathy, and practical skills, we have the power to make a difference in the lives of the youth around us. We have the opportunity to create environments of understanding, compassion, and proactive support, where every teenager feels seen, heard, and valued.

As we conclude, let us embark on a mission of empowerment for the teenagers in our lives. Let us engage in open, honest conversations, create environments of understanding and support, and actively advocate for their holistic development. Let empathy, resilience, and compassion guide our interactions, shaping a future where every teenager thrives.

So, let us always remember that we hold high power to make a huge difference. Let us embrace the challenge and opportunity before us, knowing that by taking action, we can create a world where teenagers navigate adolescence with confidence.

Now, as we conclude, we invite you to share your thoughts and reflections on our journey together. Your feedback is invaluable as we strive to create a future where teenagers thrive in mind, body, and spirit. Thank you for your participation, and we look forward to hearing from you.

Please Take a moment to scan the QR code below
and leave a review

"Kind words can be short and easy to speak, but their echoes are truly endless." - Heidi R

References

5 ways to be an active listener for your teen. (2020, September 15). Newport Academy. https://www.newportacademy.com/resources/empowering-teens/active-listener/

5 ways to help teens build self-awareness. (2014, May 2). Time for Excellence. https://lifesmartblog.com/2014/05/02/5-ways-to-help-teens-build-self-awareness/

8 tips for teens with social anxiety. (2018, February 22). CBT Psychology. https://cbtpsychology.com/7-tips-teens-with-social-anxiety/

11 facts about cyberbullying . (2019). Do Something. https://www.dosomething.org/us/facts/11-facts-about-cyber-bullying

12 ways to start meaningful conversations with your teen. (2022, February 4). GT Scholars. https://gtscholars.org/12-ways-to-start-meaningful-conversations-with-your-teen

21 cybersecurity tips and best practices for four Business [Infographic]. (2021, August 16). TitanFile. https://www.titanfile.com/blog/cyber-security-tips-best-practices/

35 social anxiety quotes. (n.d.). Conquer Social Anxiety. https://www.conquersocialanxiety.com/quotes/

Akpan, E. (2023, June 2). Healthy living in a digital age: How to protect your wellbeing amid screen time overload. CloudClinic. https://cloudclinic.ng/healthy-living-in-a-digital-age-how-to-protect-your-wellbeing-amid-screen-time-overload/

Alan Kay quotes. (n.d.). Brainy Quote. https://www.brainyquote.com/quotes/alan_kay_451980

Anderson, M. (2018, September 27). A Majority of teens have experienced some form of cyberbullying. Pew Research Center: Internet, Science & Tech; Pew Research Center. https://www.pewresearch.org/internet/2018/09/27/a-majority-of-teens-have-experienced-some-form-of-cyberbullying/

Anderson, M., & Jiang, J. (2018, November 28). Teens and their experiences on social media. Pew Research Center: Internet, Science & Tech. https://www.pewresearch.org/internet/2018/11/28/teens-and-their-experiences-on-social-media/

Anna Maria Chavez Quotes. (n.d.). BrainyQuote. https://www.brainyquote.com/quotes/anna_maria_chavez_520052

Asian American Therapists. (2023, October 13). Empowering teens in self-management skills. Yellow Chair Collective.

https://yellowchaircollective.com/nurturing-independence-
empowering-teens-to-establish-self-management-skills/

Bachert, A. (2022, April 18). 5 depressive disorders in teens
and young adults. Charlie Health.
https://www.charliehealth.com/post/5-depressive-disorders-
in-teens-and-young-adults

Balasundaram, A. (2023, November 16). Adapting digital
skills: Navigating technological advancements for students.
Linkedin. https://www.linkedin.com/pulse/adapting-digital-
skills-navigating-technological-balasundaram-
wqcye?utm_source=share&utm_medium=member_android
&utm_campaign=share_via

Beyond likes and filters: Nurturing healthy a body image in
the digital world. (n.d.). Saferkidsonline.eset.com.
https://saferkidsonline.eset.com/uk/article/beyond-likes-and-
filters-nurturing-healthy-a-body-image-in-the-digital-world

Body dysmorphic disorder (BDD) and youth. (n.d.). Mental
Health America. https://www.mhanational.org/body-
dysmorphic-disorder-bdd-and-youth

Body dysmorphic disorder (for parents). (2018). Kidshealth.
https://kidshealth.org/en/parents/bdd.html

Body image: Pre-teens and teenagers. (2017, February 2).
Raising Children. https://raisingchildren.net.au/pre-
teens/healthy-lifestyle/body-image/body-image-teens

Bruce, D. F. (2022, April 24). Teen depression: Causes, symptoms, heredity, and treatments. WebMD. https://www.webmd.com/depression/teen-depression

Cammarata, C. (2017). About teen suicide (for parents). Kids Health. https://kidshealth.org/en/parents/suicide.html

Ceder, J. (2019). How inconsistent parenting can cause behavior problems. Verywell Family. https://www.verywellfamily.com/why-does-consistency-matter-in-parenting-4135227

What to do when your child is cyberbullied: Top ten tips for parents.(2018, June 1). Cyberbullying Research Center. https://cyberbullying.org/what-to-do-when-your-child-is-cyberbullied

Cherry, K. (2022, October 13). How social comparison theory influences our views on ourselves. Verywell Mind. https://www.verywellmind.com/what-is-the-social-comparison-process-2795872

Children's Bureau. (2019, March 22). The importance of a community for teenagers. Child Abuse Prevention, Treatment & Welfare Services | Children's Bureau. https://www.all4kids.org/news/blog/the-importance-of-a-community-for-teenagers/

Comparison: Thief of joy. (n.d.). Disability Is Natural. https://www.disabilityisnatural.com/comparison.html

Coping Strategies For Body Dysmorphic Disorder (BDD) -
Klarity Health Library. (2023, August 23).
https://my.klarity.health/coping-strategies-for-body-
dysmorphic-disorder/

Cuncic, A. (2020, September 19). 7 types of social fears and
the best way to overcome them. Verywell Mind.
https://www.verywellmind.com/practice-social-anxiety-
disorder-exposure-therapy-3024845

Cyberbullying: The mental health impact and how to help
your teen. (2023, January 18). Newport Academy.
https://www.newportacademy.com/resources/restoring-
families/teen-
cyberbullying/#:~:text=In%20one%20study%2C%2093%20pe
rcent

Dam, K. (n.d.). 5 core reasons you should keep up with
technology trends. Kand.io. https://kand.io/blog/5-core-
reasons-you-should-keep-up-with-technology-trends

Daze, G. (2022, May 2). Environmental depression risk
factors and impacts. BrainsWay.
https://www.brainsway.com/knowledge-
center/environmental-factors-and-depression/

Depression in children. (2020, November 17). Cleveland
Clinic. https://my.clevelandclinic.org/health/diseases/14938-
depression-in-children

Depression in young people. (2023, January 14). Health Direct. https://www.healthdirect.gov.au/depression-in-young-people

Depression treatment for teens and young adults. (n.d.). Paradigm Treatment. https://paradigmtreatment.com/teen-treatment/depression/

Depression treatments for children and adolescents. (2021). American Psychological Association. https://www.apa.org/depression-guideline/children-and-adolescents

Destinations. (2022, October 26). 10 common causes of anxiety in teens. Destinations for Teens Mental Health Treatment Center. https://www.destinationsforteens.com/destinations-blog/10-common-causes-of-anxiety-in-teens/

Digital citizenship: teens being responsible online. (2018, December 20). Raising Children Network. https://raisingchildren.net.au/pre-teens/entertainment-technology/digital-life/digital-citizenship

Digital content — finding, evaluating, using and creating it. (n.d.). Natlib. https://natlib.govt.nz/schools/digital-literacy/strategies-for-developing-digital-literacy/digital-content-finding-evaluating-using-and-creating-it

Does your teen seem depressed? Here's how to help. (2019). Verywell Mind. https://www.verywellmind.com/initial-steps-in-helping-your-depressed-teen-2609493

Dutta, S. (2022, March 28). Eating disorders and social media. News Medical Life Sciences. https://www.news-medical.net/health/Eating-Disorders-and-Social-Media.aspx

Eating disorders. (2023, January). National Institute of Mental Health. https://www.nimh.nih.gov/health/topics/eating-disorders

Education-teen suicide. (n.d.). Department of Mental Health. https://dmh.lacounty.gov/our-services/employment-education/education/teen-suicide/#:~:text=Some%20Suicide%20Statistics&text=It%20is%20estimated%20that%20depression

Ellis, A. K. D., Davis, A. K., & Ellis, S. (2024, March 23). These celeb parents have shared their social media & technology Rules for Their Kids. SheKnows. https://www.sheknows.com/parenting/slideshow/2706813/celebrity-parents-technology-rules/3/

Embracing your inner beauty: Tips for feeling beautiful inside and out. (n.d.). Clever Little. https://heycleverlittle.com/blogs/news/embracing-your-inner-beauty-tips-for-feeling-beautiful-inside-and-out

Gerten, K. (2021, March 17). It's hard. 13 quotes that illustrate depression. Youth Dynamic. https://www.youthdynamics.org/its-hard-13-quotes-that-illustrate-depression/

Gluck, S. (2013). Quotes on eating disorders. Healthyplace. https://www.healthyplace.com/insight/quotes/quotes-on-eating-disorders

Gordon, S. (2022, July 22). What are the effects of cyberbullying? Verywell Family. https://www.verywellfamily.com/what-are-the-effects-of-cyberbullying-460558

Goyal, S., Srivastava, K., & Bansal, V. (2009). Study of prevalence of depression in adolescent students of a public school. Industrial Psychiatry Journal, 18(1), 43. https://doi.org/10.4103/0972-6748.57859

Gray, P. (2023, November 19). Benefits and challenges of social media use for teens. Psychology Today.https://www.psychologytoday.com/us/blog/freedom-to-learn/202311/benefits-and-challenges-of-social-media-use-for-teens

Grinspoon, P. (2022, May 4). How to recognize and tame your cognitive distortions. Harvard Health. https://www.health.harvard.edu/blog/how-to-recognize-and-tame-your-cognitive-distortions-202205042738

Help and advice for parents. (n.d.). https://bddfoundation.org/support/supporting-someone-with-bdd/help-and-advice-for-parents/

Hieber, B. (2016, October 10). Teenagers now and then. The growl. https://medium.com/thegrowl/teenagers-now-and-then-f3aec8a974c4

Holland, K. (2014, November 26). Eating disorders: Causes and risk factors. Healthline Media. https://www.healthline.com/health/eating-disorders-causes-risk-factors

How social media affects mental health: The effects of constant connectivity. (2022, October 24). Mile High Psychiatry. https://milehighpsychiatry.com/how-social-media-affects-mental-health-the-effects-of-constant-connectivity/

How to create a safe environment for your teen. (2017, January 25). Paradigm Treatment. https://paradigmtreatment.com/create-safe-environment-teen/

How to Have a Conversation More Easily When You Have SAD. (n.d.). Verywell Mind. https://www.verywellmind.com/talk-people-social-anxiety-disorder-3024390

How to spot someone with an eating disorder. (n.d.). Lifeworks community. https://www.lifeworkscommunity.com/eating-disorders-treatment/how-to-recognise-the-early-signs-of-an-eating-disorder

Institute Staff. (2021, May 10). The importance of being open and honest with your kids. ICP. https://www.childhoodpreparedness.org/post/the-importance-of-being-open-and-honest-with-your-kids

It broke my heart to see my son suffer from social anxiety. (2020, March 5). Parenting teens and tweens.com. https://parentingteensandtweens.com/how-to-help-your-teen-with-social-anxiety/

Kapil, R. (2019, July 11). Four ways culture impacts mental health. Mental Health First Aid. https://www.mentalhealthfirstaid.org/2019/07/four-ways-culture-impacts-mental-health/

Katella, K. (2024, January 8). How social media affects your teen's mental health: A parent's guide. Yale Medicine; Yale Medicine. https://www.yalemedicine.org/news/social-media-teen-mental-health-a-parents-guide

Kevorkian, M. (2019). Parents can prevent cyberbullying. PTA. https://www.pta.org/home/family-resources/safety/Digital-Safety/Parents-Can-Prevent-Cyberbullying

Lakhwani, S. (2023, September 15). Fundamentals of cybersecurity: Getting your basics right. Knowledge Hut. https://www.knowledgehut.com/blog/security/cyber-security-fundamentals

What is digital literacy: Definition and uses in daily life. (2023, January 26). Learning. https://www.learning.com/blog/what-is-digital-literacy-definition-and-uses-in-daily-life/

LCSW-C, E. K. (2021, December 21). Social anxiety in teens: Signs & symptoms. Talk space. https://www.talkspace.com/blog/social-anxiety-in-teens/

Liles, M. (2021, January 29). These 50 inspirational quotes for family caregivers will get you through tough days. Parade: Entertainment, Recipes, Health, Life, Holidays. https://parade.com/1004993/marynliles/caregiver-quotes/

Lyness, D. (2019). Eating disorders (for teens). Kids health. https://kidshealth.org/en/teens/eat-disorder.html

Masjedi, Y. (2022, April 22). How to protect your privacy online (With 10 examples). Www.aura.com. https://www.aura.com/learn/how-to-protect-your-privacy-online

Mayo Clinic. (2017, July 14). Eating disorder treatment: Know your options. Mayo Clinic. https://www.mayoclinic.org/diseases-conditions/eating-disorders/in-depth/eating-disorder-treatment/art-20046234

Melinda. (2019, March 21). HelpGuide.org. Help Guide. https://www.helpguide.org/articles/parenting-family/family-caregiving.htm

Mental health of adolescents. (2021, November 17). World Health Organization. https://www.who.int/news-room/fact-sheets/detail/adolescent-mental-health

Mikhail, A. (2022, November 3). TikToks with billions of views spread harmful and false messages about body image to young people. How parents can intervene. Fortune. https://fortune.com/well/2022/11/03/tiktoks-spread-harmful-and-false-messages-about-body-image-to-young-people/

Miller, C. (2022, October 11). How anxiety affects teenagers. Child Mind Institute. https://childmind.org/article/signs-of-anxiety-in-teenagers/

Mojtabai, R., Olfson, M., & Han, B. (2016). National trends in the prevalence and treatment of depression in adolescents and young adults. Pediatrics, 138(6), e20161878–e20161878. https://doi.org/10.1542/peds.2016-1878

More time on social media increases the risk of cyberbullying. (2021, April 22). Evolve Treatment Centers. https://evolvetreatment.com/blog/social-media-cyberbullying/

Muhlheim, L. (2019). Why do some people get eating disorders? Verywell Mind. https://www.verywellmind.com/what-causes-eating-disorders-4121047

Nienau, J. (2019, November 21). How social comparison bias is affecting us and what we can do about it. The Post-Grad Survival Guide. https://medium.com/the-post-grad-survival-guide/how-social-comparison-bias-is-affecting-us-and-what-we-can-do-about-it-d9984cb5e43a

Osorio, E. K., & Hyde, E. (2021). The rise of anxiety and depression among young adults in the United States. Ballard

Brief. https://ballardbrief.byu.edu/issue-briefs/the-rise-of-anxiety-and-depression-among-young-adults-in-the-united-states

Pedersen, T. (2023, February 27). How does social media affect body image? Psych Central; Psych Central. https://psychcentral.com/health/how-the-media-affects-body-image

Planned parenthood. (2019). Planned Parenthood. https://www.plannedparenthood.org/learn/teens/bullying-safety-privacy/bullying/bullying-social-media

Pontz, E. (2018, September 4). Creating safe boundaries for teens to push against. Center for Parent and Teen Communication. https://parentandteen.com/creating-safe-boundaries/

Practicing gratitude can benefit kids' mental health. (2022, December 27). CHOC - Children's Health Hub. https://health.choc.org/practicing-gratitude-can-benefit-kids-mental-health/

Preventing cyberbullying. (2020). Delete Cyberbullying. https://www.endcyberbullying.net/preventing-cyberbullying

Rapaport, L. (2019, December 14). Social media use linked to teen disordered eating behaviors. Reuters. https://www.reuters.com/article/idUSKBN1YH2GF/

Regoniel, P. (2023, November 16). How do you protect your privacy online? 6 ways. Simply Educate. https://simplyeducate.me/2023/11/16/how-do-you-protect-your-privacy-online/

Riehm, K. E., Feder, K. A., Tormohlen, K. N., Crum, R. M., Young, A. S., Green, K. M., Pacek, L. R., La Flair, L. N., & Mojtabai, R. (2019). Associations between time spent using social media and internalizing and externalizing problems among US youth. JAMA Psychiatry, 76(12), 1266–1273. https://doi.org/10.1001/jamapsychiatry.2019.2325

Saeed, M. (2023, June 12). Embracing authenticity: Overcoming psychological barriers to self-acceptance. LinkedIn. https://www.linkedin.com/pulse/embracing-authenticity-overcoming-psychological-barriers-marina-saeed?utm_source=share&utm_medium=member_android&utm_campaign=share_via

Securly. (2023, October 4). The 10 types of cyberbullying. Blog. https://blog.securly.com/the-10-types-of-cyberbullying/

Self care: Cultivating wellness in everyday life. (n.d.). Gray group intl. https://www.graygroupintl.com/blog/self-care

Self-compassion for pre-teens and teenagers. (n.d.). Raising Children Network. https://raisingchildren.net.au/teens/mental-health-physical-health/about-mental-health/self-compassion-teenagers

Sherrell, Z. (2021, September 15). Social media and mental health: Depression and psychological effects. Medical news today. https://www.medicalnewstoday.com/articles/social-media-and-mental-health#statistics

Signs and symptoms. (n.d.). Eatingdisorderfoundation.org. https://eatingdisorderfoundation.org/learn-more/about-eating-disorders/signs-and-symptoms/

Social comparison theory. (2019). Psychology Today. https://www.psychologytoday.com/us/basics/social-comparison-theory

Solomon, D. (2022, March 9). Social media has made beauty unattainable. Next Generation Politics. https://www.nextgenpolitics.org/blog/social-media-beauty

Suicide. (2018, December 20). HelpGuide. https://www.helpguide.org/articles/depression/parents-guide-to-teen-depression.htm

Teen depression signs & symptoms. (n.d.). Newport Academy. https://www.newportacademy.com/teen-depression/signs-symptoms/

The hidden consequences of constant social comparison. (2023, November 6). Impossible Psychological Services. https://www.impossiblepsychservices.com.sg/our-resources/articles/2023/11/06/the-hidden-consequences-of-constant-social-comparison

The impact of technology on teens' mental wellness. (2021, March 6). Clarity Child Guidance Center. https://www.claritycgc.org/too-much-of-a-good-thing-the-impact-of-technology-on-teens-mental-wellness/

The long-term effects of cyberbullying. (2016, December 11). US Represented. https://usrepresented.com/2016/12/10/the-long-term-effects-of-cyberbullying/

Thiefels, J. (2019, March 27). What every teen needs to know about their digital footprint. Net Nanny. https://www.netnanny.com/blog/what-every-teen-needs-to-know-about-their-digital-footprint/

Top 21 body dysmorphia quotes that will make you feel less alone. (2022, November 12). https://ineffableliving.com/body-dysmorphia-quotes/

Valkama, P. (2013, October 25). Invisible online: How anonymity affects cyberbullying. Trulioo. https://www.trulioo.com/blog/identity-verification/invisible-online-how-anonymity-affects-cyberbullying

Walsh, S. (2023, November 6). The top 10 social media sites & platforms. Search Engine Journal. https://www.searchenginejournal.com/social-media/social-media-platforms/

Warrender, D., & Milne, R. (2020, February 24). How use of social media and social comparison affect mental health. Nursing Times. https://www.nursingtimes.net/news/mental-health/how-use-of-social-media-and-social-comparison-affect-mental-health-24-02-2020/

Ways to build trust between parents and teens. (2022, June 17). Boys & Girls Clubs of America. https://www.bgca.org/news-stories/2022/June/ways-to-build-trust-between-parents-and-teens/

Wei, M. (2018, October 17). Self-care for the caregiver. Harvard Health Blog. https://www.health.harvard.edu/blog/self-care-for-the-caregiver-2018101715003

What causes depression? (2023). In Centre for Clinical Interventions. https://www.cci.health.wa.gov.au/~/media/CCI/Mental-Health-Professionals/Depression/Depression---Information-Sheets/Depression-Information-Sheet---02---What-Causes-Depression.pdf

What's one thing parents don't understand about teenagers? (2019). Quora. https://www.quora.com/Whats-one-thing-parents-dont-understand-about-teenagers

Why is self-awareness important for teens? (2021, November 15). Stone Water Recovery. https://www.stonewaterrecovery.com/adolescent-treatment-blog/why-is-self-awareness-important-for-teens?hs_amp=true

Williams, R. (n.d.). 5 social media trends that parents need to know about in 2023: Part 1. Smart about Social.

https://www.smartaboutsocial.com/blog/social-media-trends-virtual-followers

Yassin, F. (2021, December 10). 5 reasons why teenagers are suffering from anxiety disorder more than ever before. The Wave Clinic. https://thewaveclinic.com/blog/5-reasons-why-teenagers-are-suffering-from-anxiety-disorder-more-than-ever-before/

Your adolescent: Anxiety and avoidant disorders. (2019). American Academy of Child & Adolescent Psychiatry. https://www.aacap.org/aacap/Families_and_Youth/Resource_Centers/Anxiety_Disorder_Resource_Center/Your_Adolescent_Anxiety_and_Avoidant_Disorders.aspx

Made in the USA
Las Vegas, NV
27 May 2024